SELL
YOURSELF
IN ANY
INTERVIEW

SELL YOURSELF IN ANY INTERVIEW

Use Proven Sales Techniques to Land Your Dream Job

OSCAR ADLER

New York   Chicago   San Francisco   Lisbon
London   Madrid   Mexico City   Milan
New Delhi   San Juan   Seoul
Singapore   Sydney   Toronto

1 2 3 4 5 6 7 8 9 0 FGR/FGR 0 9 8

ISBN   978-0-07-154909-7
MHID 0-07-154909-9

McGraw-Hill books are available at special quantity discounts to use as premiums and sales promotions, or for use in corporate training programs. To contact a representative please visit the Contact Us pages at www.mh professional.com.

This book is printed on acid-free paper.

Library of Congress Cataloging-in-Publication Data

Adler, Oscar.
  Sell yourself in any interview : use proven sales techniques
to land your dream job / by Oscar Adler.
      p. cm.
  Includes bibliographical references and index.
  ISBN 0-07-154909-9 (alk. paper)
  1. Employment interviewing. I. Title.

HF5549.5.I6A35 2008
650.14'4—dc22   2007044510

Contents

Acknowledgments   vii

Introduction   ix

CHAPTER 1   The Power of Features and Benefits   1

CHAPTER 2   Addressing Each Interviewer's Individual Needs   15

CHAPTER 3   Listen Better to Learn What's Important to Each Interviewer   41

CHAPTER 4   Asking Questions with Skill and Finesse   63

CHAPTER 5   Answering Questions with Outstanding Benefits   85

CHAPTER 6   Getting and Maximizing References and Referrals   107

CHAPTER 7   How to Prepare for Different Interview Situations   117

CHAPTER 8   The Interview—Before, During, and After   137

Index   155

Acknowledgments

First, I'd like to thank Illinois State Senator Susan Garrett, who, after sponsoring and attending one of my seminars for job seekers, "strongly suggested" that I write a book on the subjects I discussed at the seminar, and she continued urging me until I did it. Obviously, this book would not be available today were it not for her; Susan, I sincerely thank you for all you did.

I owe a special thank you to Susan Bearman, whose expertise, intelligence, judgment, and writing skills were extremely important to the book-writing effort.

I also would like to thank my agent, Ruth Mills, who has a formidable array of personal assets that were of exceptional help, not to mention her wonderful patience with me.

Thanks also to Dr. Robert Brawer, who gave me considerable confidence and insight in writing this book. I am also very grateful to him because he introduced me to Ruth Mills.

Derek Ragona, my computer guru, and more, was invaluable in helping with all the important technological aspects involved with making this book a reality.

One of the best critics anyone could have on a book-writing project is Edgar Rose. He gave much of his valuable time reviewing and evaluating material that hopefully will benefit many job seekers.

And none of the preceding would have happened if my wife Norma was not involved. She was an editor, contributor, and proofreader. Above all, she had the fortitude, desire, and patience to put up with all my moods, idiosyncrasies, and doubts. She is wonderful.

Introduction

································

Every week, 2.5 million new people become job seekers and face the daunting task of interviewing for a job. In fact, statistics show that most Americans will change jobs upwards of 10 times during their careers—which means that they endure at least 10 job-related interviews, and this doesn't include some jobs that require more than one interview! Here's another sobering fact: The average job search takes between three and nine months.

But you don't care about how difficult it is for everyone else to get a job; all you care about is getting *your* next job. This book can help you because it's different from the dozens of other job-hunting guides on library and bookstore shelves in two important ways. First, most of the so-called experts who wrote those other books have *never actually hired anyone*. Some are lawyers or academics, whereas others are career coaches who take an outsider's point of view. Many are human resources specialists who play a gate-keeping role during the job-hunting process but who *aren't the ultimate decision makers*.

In contrast, as a sales and training manager, I have conducted thousands of interviews and hired hundreds of people over my 40-year career—and I know what interviewers want. I have been in the position of the hiring manager (many, many times!), having to choose the best person for the job—and holding the fate of the interviewee in my hands. In my consulting practice, I have trained hundreds of people to become successful at the art of the interview. I have worked with people at every career phase, from entry-level jobs to top positions at major corporations. No matter what job level you are seeking, I can help you to answer the question: "What will you do for *me*?"

In these pages I won't simply tell you to feel relaxed and be confident—I will show you how. I won't simply tell you to sell yourself—I will teach you proven techniques for selling your most important product—you.

Still don't think my techniques can work for you? Think again. As part of my consulting practice, I provide pro bono workshops for soon-to-be-released convicts who must, as a condition of parole, become active job hunters. If I can teach ex-cons how to sell themselves in a job interview, I know I can help *you* be successful, too.

The second reason this book is different is because every other book available puts the focus in the wrong place. Not one single job-hunting guide explains how to identify the needs and desires of individual companies and interviewers. More important, no one tells you how to present your skills and experiences to address those needs and desires. Even more important than that, no one tells you how to answer the interviewer's underlying (but often unspoken) question: "What will you do for *me*?"

Have you ever thought about what an interviewer might be thinking during a job interview? Probably not. You are most likely thinking about what *you* should say and do. This is the most common mistake people make on job interviews— they concentrate on themselves instead of on the interviewer. I can hear you ask: "But isn't it all about *me*?" No! It's all about what the *interviewer* wants and needs. So what is the interviewer thinking, you ask? Even though he or she may never speak it aloud, the interviewer is most likely thinking about the six most important words in any job interview— "What will you do for *me*?"

WHAT THIS BOOK WILL DO FOR YOU

I wrote this book for you—the job hunter—not for academics or human resources professionals. You won't find heavy-handed explanations, boring statistics, or thousands of for-mulaic answers for you to memorize. Most job-hunting guides either provide advice that is *too general*, telling you to "feel confident" and "sell yourself" without giving you the specifics of how to achieve these vagaries, or are *too specific*, presenting hundreds of questions and answers and expecting you somehow to memorize all of them.

In contrast, this book will teach you the skills to learn, practice, and use in your very next interview. Each chapter will briefly discuss the general concepts you need to know, offer a variety of real-life examples, and take you through practical exercises that show you specifically how to apply the lessons in job-hunting situations. It will serve as your *work-book*, not some long lecture about job hunting. Each chapter is devoted to a specific skill, and you are encouraged to move at your own pace. Along the way, you will be challenged to complete ability-strengthening worksheets, practicing each new skill and, finally, rating yourself before moving on to the next step. These self-assessments will reassure you that you have achieved a level of competency, while building your con-fidence as you go. For example, in Chapter 8, the "Interview Review Form" provides you with a consistent method for evaluating your performance after each interview, helping you to hone the skills that work best and develop strategies for making improvements where you falter.

Many interview guides expect you to memorize hundreds of answers, claiming that they will guarantee success when, in fact, trying to sound like someone else dooms you to fail-ure. You don't need to memorize other people's words to succeed in an interview. In fact, using your own words and style will make you feel more comfortable, capable, and confident—and these are the qualities that shine through during an interview. In this book you will learn skills, not style.

Experienced interviewers have told me that they can spot a "canned" answer right away and that it always makes a negative impression. The interviewer wants to get to know *you*—what you think and what you have to offer—and will not appreciate it when you simply spout off the answers you read in some book. I'll prove to you that the only answers that will guarantee your success are the ones that are meaningful to the interviewer.

My skills-based approach will teach you the strategies employed every day by successful salespeople, including

❑ The power of features and benefits—and how you need to emphasize the benefits of hiring *you* during every interview

❑ How to recognize and address each interviewer's individual needs

❑ How to translate your own features into benefits that are meaningful to each person interviewing you

❑ Important strategies for becoming a good listener—and why listening is vital to a successful job search

❑ How to ask questions skillfully and answer questions with outstanding benefits that (again) show why *you* are the candidate the interviewer should hire

❑ How to get and maximize references and referrals

❑ How to prepare for different interview situations—from interviews with headhunters, human resources, hiring managers, and prospective coworkers to a variety of interview situations, including meal interviews, group interviews, and "elevator" interviews where you have only a few minutes to sell yourself

❏ A review of everything you need to know before the interview and on the day of your interview and what to do after you get the job offer you want

You will learn to recognize the question "What will you do for *me*?" in all its guises. If a human resources person says, "Tell me about yourself," you will understand that he or she is really asking: "What do you have to offer that I can show the hiring manager?"

If a hiring manager asks, "What are your greatest strengths?" you will recognize that the real question is, "What will you bring to the table that will make my team more successful, thereby making me look good?" If a company vice president asks, "Where do you see yourself in five years?" you will know that the question he or she is secretly looking to have answered is, "Do you have career aspirations and ambitions that will justify my investment in hiring you so that I stay on budget and meet the goals of my division?"

Most important, you will learn that the critical part of answering these silent questions that run through the mind of every interviewer is to end with a *benefit* that is meaningful to each specific individual—which helps you get the job you want.

MAKING THE MOST OF YOUR INVESTMENT

As you probably know, a job search can be a long, difficult, and frustrating process. It starts with your own needs and wants, strengths and weaknesses, and experience. Then you translate those strengths and experiences into the perfect résumé. Next comes extensive research on industries, companies, positions, and individuals. You make contacts, answer ads, work with headhunters, and follow up on leads. You invest in wardrobes, haircuts, and briefcases. And after all this time and effort, it all comes down to the interview. That's a big investment of time, money, and energy. This book will help to maximize that investment and turn the interview into a job offer.

You can spend hundreds of hours preparing for a half-hour interview. Although the interview itself actually occurs fairly late in the job-hunting process, if you fail during the interview, all the hard work you have done goes to waste. You will learn to make the most of those 30 minutes, providing answers that meet the needs and wants of the interviewer.

I'm not promising that you will get a job offer from every interview you have. But don't be afraid to fail: After all, baseball players with a .300 batting average are still failing 7 out of 10 times at bat—and they're considered stars who make millions of dollars. The reason they succeed is because they don't quit; instead, they continue to practice their skills over and over again. And if you practice the skills presented here, you too will learn from your mistakes and turn failure into success.

My objective is to make your interviewing experience successful, employing a set of specific skills that will enable you to use your own words to their maximum effect. As mentioned earlier, the information here has evolved from years of conducting training seminars. Each session of my workshop is devoted to a specific skill, and I encourage attendees to go home and practice each one. Therefore, this book is not meant to be read cover to cover in one sitting. Instead, each chapter addresses what I cover in each of my training sessions, and I suggest that you work through the book one chapter at a time, just as if you were attending one of my workshops. Take time to complete the worksheets, practice each new skill, and rate yourself honestly at the end of each chapter before you move on to the next one.

LIFELONG SKILLS, LIFELONG BENEFITS

In addition to using these skills in job interviews, the skills you will learn here can be applied directly to performance reviews and requests for promotions and raises. In short, these skills will be invaluable to you throughout your career.

Work your way through these eight chapters and you will learn to answer, with confidence, the question: "What will you do for *me*?" That confidence will lead to success—in your interview, in the resulting new job, and in all your professional and interpersonal communications.

CHAPTER 1

The Power of Features and Benefits

*Nothing is more pleasing and engaging
than the sense of having conferred benefits.
Not even the gratification of receiving them.*

—Ellis Peters, AUTHOR

The key to a successful job interview is to convince the interviewer that by hiring you, he will benefit directly. Sure, the skills, expertise, and experience you bring are important. Personality also plays a role, but the thing that will get you hired is your ability to show interviewers how you will benefit *them*.

I did not invent the idea of *features* and *benefits*; in fact, you have probably heard the terms in many contexts before. For our purposes, a *feature* is a unique, inherent quality. A *benefit* is the pleasure or satisfaction someone gets from a given feature. Few people know how to use benefits to their advantage—in daily life or in a job interview. The *benefit* in a job interview is the answer to the question: "What will you do for *me*?" It is the answer *you* need to give to get the job you want.

1

I'll return to this concept of features and benefits throughout this book. You will see how using feature/benefit skills effectively can lead to success in your job search, as well as improve your communications skills in every area of your life.

SELLING IS TELLING

Features and benefits are key concepts in sales. Selling is nothing more than *telling* with a purpose. I know that for most people the idea of *sales* is a scary thought. I can hear you saying: "But I'm a teacher, not a salesperson. I don't want to be in sales." Don't panic over the word. The fact is that we are all in sales. We all sell every day. For example, if you are a teacher, you sell ideas, facts, theories, methods, and strategies to your students all the time. You may not think of it as selling, but it really is. You are *telling* your students the *facts* (or *features*) of a given topic, but you are *showing* them the *benefits* of learning about that topic. You are making it relevant to them. Successful teachers are great salespeople. So are successful lawyers, graphic designers, computer programmers, and tour guides.

Our world becomes more competitive by the day, and elements of sales have crept into every industry. Successful people use sales techniques to seek out and retain clients, to convince a boss to make an investment, or simply to maintain a competitive edge. In nonprofit and fund-raising organizations, staff members often have to sell ideas to their board members, supporters, or politicians. Even in organizations that seem far removed from the world of sales, you still need to be able to sell *yourself* during an annual review or when asking for a raise.

Certainly we can agree that the act of finding a new job involves sales. You are the product, and the hiring manager is the customer. Whenever you are looking for a job—whether it is your first full-time job after graduation, a new job that will move you forward in your existing career, or a job in a completely new field—you need to sell yourself.

In sales, we *start* with the features of a product or service and *end* with its benefits. Ending with the benefit is essential. The last thing you say is the thing that people remember most. In perhaps the simplest example, most parents quickly learn this lesson, ending their statements with a benefit that is meaningful to the child: "After you eat your dinner, you may have a cookie."

When interviewing for a job, you need to present the *features* (i.e., skills and experience) you have to offer and highlight them by ending your statements with the *benefits* those features will have for a prospective employer. You need to end every statement by answering the interviewer's real question: "What will you do for *me*?"

During my many years as a sales executive and career coach, I have discovered that few people understand the importance of using feature/benefit skills as part of their business or personal communication repertoires. Some have indicated that they "sort of knew about" features and benefits, but they never really learned how to use them. Attendees of my job-hunting workshops tell me how helpful understanding feature/benefit skills can be and that they felt empowered when they saw the skills at work.

UNDERSTANDING THE DIFFERENCE BETWEEN FEATURES AND BENEFITS

The difference between a feature and a benefit may seem subtle at first. Once again, a feature is simply a trait—a fact.

In contrast, a benefit is something that aids or promotes well-being. A benefit can be thought of as the *result* of a feature—in other words, it is *because* of this feature that you are getting this benefit. By the end of this chapter you will be able to distinguish the difference between a feature and a benefit, state features clearly, and end each statement with a related benefit.

Let's start with a simple example—a yellow pencil. One feature might be that "a pencil writes." A benefit might be: "This pencil allows me to express myself in writing."

Exhibit 1-1 FEATURE AND BENEFIT QUIZ

Read the statements below and indicate whether you think each one is a feature or a benefit. Use the letter **F** for feature and the letter **B** for benefit.

- This automobile has heated seats. _____

- This copier makes 30 clean copies in one minute. _____

- This is a full-service insurance company. _____

- These potatoes were grown organically. _____

- The hose on this vacuum cleaner stretches to twice its normal length. _____

- This carpet comes with a 10-year warranty. _____

- Our health club has an indoor track. _____

- I have a master's degree in business administration. _____

- I have been a paralegal for 10 years. _____

Similarly, an eraser lets you remove pencil writing. That's a feature. A benefit might be: "The eraser lets me get rid of my mistakes."

So let's do our first exercise: See Exhibit 1-1—stop reading in order to complete the exercise now. These worksheets are vitally important because they will help you to test how much you know about effective interviewing. Once you have completed this worksheet, continue reading so that you can check your answers to gauge how well you did.

Every statement made on the list in Exhibit 1-1 is a feature. They are simply facts—they do not tell the listener the benefits of the given feature. Features without benefits do not mean very much to the interviewer. Benefits are the only thing people really care about. Remember, you are always answering the question: "What will you do for *me*?" This is the *only* thing interviewers care about. In fact, it's the only thing most people care about.

TRANSLATING FEATURES INTO BENEFITS

People do not automatically translate features into benefits when they hear them. We do not necessarily ask ourselves: "What will that feature do for *me*?" We are far more likely to think: "So what?"

An interviewer will be listening only for the benefits of hiring you. She cares only that she makes the right hiring decision. If you answer questions with features but fail to relate the benefits, you are not selling yourself to the interviewer. You must learn to highlight every answer by ending with an appropriate benefit.

It's important to note that just because someone is listening to you, even if they are listening intently, they are not necessarily hearing or understanding you. You need to become your own translator—translating the features you bring (i.e., your skills and background) into meaningful benefits for the interviewer.

As a practice exercise, read the list of features from Exhibit 1-1 and try to write a corresponding benefit for each. See Exhibit 1-2.

Exhibit 1-2 PRACTICE WORKSHEET: TRANSLATING FEATURES INTO BENEFITS

Read the following list of features from the Worksheet in Exhibit 1-1 and write a corresponding benefit for each. There is no one *right* answer; a single feature can and usually does have more than one benefit. The point of this exercise is to begin thinking in terms of benefits. (The first one has been completed for you as an example.)

Feature: This automobile has heated seats.

Benefit: _Heated seats warm you up fast on a cold winter day._

Feature: This copier makes 30 clean copies in one minute.

Benefit: _____

_____

Feature: This is a full-service insurance company.

Benefit: _____

_____

Feature: These potatoes were grown organically.

Benefit: _____

_____

Feature: The hose on this vacuum cleaner stretches to twice its normal length.

Benefit: _____

_____

Feature: This carpet comes with a 10-year warranty.

Benefit: _____

_____

Feature: Our health club has an indoor track.

Benefit: _____

_____

Feature: I have a master's degree in business administration.

Benefit: _____

_____

Feature: I have been a paralegal for 10 years.

Benefit: _____

_____

It's not as easy as it looks, is it? One reason is that a single feature can have more than one benefit. In fact, a single feature can offer many different benefits, and the benefits may change depending on the listener. Let's take another look at our list of features—in Exhibit 1-3. You'll notice that sample benefits for all the statements have been provided.

Exhibit 1-3 SAMPLE FEATURES AND BENEFITS

Feature: This automobile has heated seats.

Benefit: Heated seats warm you up faster.

Feature: This copier makes 30 clean copies in one minute.

Benefit: Fast copying allows you to get more work done.

Feature: This is a full-service insurance company.

Benefit: We can meet all your insurance needs.

Feature: These potatoes were grown organically.

Benefit: Our organic suppliers protect you and your family from the dangers of pesticides.

Feature: The hose on this vacuum cleaner stretches to twice its normal length.

Benefit: You won't have to bend down as often to plug it in and unplug it as you move from room to room.

Feature: This carpet comes with a 10-year warranty.

Benefit: Our replacement policy protects your investment from stains and fading.

Feature: Our health club has an indoor track.

Benefit: You can exercise safely in any weather at any time of day or night.

Feature: I have a master's degree in business administration.

Benefit: My education will allow me to implement the latest research in best business practices for your organization.

Feature: I have been a paralegal for 10 years.

Benefit: My experience will allow me to step in and be productive for you on day one.

Now take a minute to compare your sample benefits (from Exhibit 1-2) with the ones shown in Exhibit 1-3. Have you truly stated a benefit, or have you merely listed another feature? Let's take a closer look at one of the examples:

Feature: "This automobile has heated seats."

What benefit could we offer to a potential customer that is related to this feature? The temptation is to say something like, "They are comfortable." Although *comfortable* may seem like a benefit, it is in fact another feature. Simply throwing an adjective into a sentence does not make it a benefit. In this case, a benefit would be

"These leather seats have a two-level heating system, so even in the coldest weather you will feel comfortable quickly."

Saying that the seats "are comfortable" is stating a feature; showing how the heated leather seats will help the customer "feel comfortable" is giving a benefit. Once you can see a feature through the eyes of a customer, then it will become clear how to state a corresponding benefit.

In the context of a job interview, the interviewer is your customer. Keep this in mind as we take another look at the final two examples in Exhibits 1-2 and 1-3, which are specifically related to the job search. In example 8, our new graduate's feature is a master's degree in business administration (MBA). The corresponding benefit is bringing current research into play at the interviewer's company. In example 9, our paralegal has the feature of 10 years' experience, and the benefit is the ability to be productive immediately.

COMBINING FEATURES WITH BENEFITS

It takes practice to combine features and benefits into one smooth statement, and this ability is crucial in presenting benefits effectively. For example, you may not want to say, "This automobile has heated seats, *so the benefit would be* a warm tush." This sounds clunky and awkward. It doesn't make the listener say to herself, "I must have heated seats!" By learning to express the benefit smoothly and seamlessly at the end of a statement, your listener will be able to picture in her mind's eye exactly what that feature will do for her. For example:

> "On a cold winter day, our heated seats warm you up fast and keep you comfortable."

Keep practicing the skill of presenting a feature with a benefit at the end of your sentence. Here are a few more examples:

❑ "I have supervised a department of 10 employees and can help you to build a cooperative, efficient team."

❑ "I have edited and produced a variety of written materials, which will allow me to get your company's message out in any format or venue."

❑ "I know the curriculum standards for grades K through 8 and can step into an opening at any grade level."

MAKE IT A HABIT TO TALK ABOUT BENEFITS

To become truly efficient at using features and benefits, you need to make it a habit. Habits are those things we do automatically, without thinking. Habits can be useful, such as exercising regularly; they can be destructive, such as smoking; or they can be neutral—for example, right-handers tend to put on their right sock first. Changing an old habit or adopting a new one is always difficult, as anyone who has ever tried to quit smoking or start exercising understands. And making a new habit frequently requires breaking an old one first.

You may be thinking: "Okay, I'll practice this benefit skill a few times, and it will become a habit." But be aware that it is not as easy to adopt a new habit as you might think. Two thousand years ago, the Roman poet Ovid wrote, "Nothing is stronger than habit." The high-pressure situation of a job interview is not the time to be practicing *anything*—especially new skills. Even the coolest candidate will revert to habit when put on the spot.

Experience has taught me that people who *regularly practice* the skill of presenting features and benefits until it becomes a habit are actually less nervous and more comfortable during an interview. You will feel more confident and in control, making you even more appealing as a potential employee.

I suggest that you post the words "What will you do for *me*?" where you can see them frequently. Make it your screen saver, or put signs around your apartment or house. The signs are a visible reminder for you to practice so that you can begin to feel comfortable using these new skills. (*Feature:* The signs remind you to practice. *Benefit:* As you practice, you will begin to feel comfortable using your new skills to become a successful interviewee.)

So how long does it take to make a new habit? Conventional wisdom says that adopting a new habit or changing an old one takes 21 to 30 days. This means that you should practice the skill of articulating features and benefits several times a day for three to four weeks before you can consider it a habit.

DOES THIS REALLY WORK?

So I hear you saying, "Okay, okay, I get it. Features and benefits. But does it really work? What will it do for *me*?" I'll give you just one example.

I was contacted by a highly qualified woman who was trying to change jobs. She had been on several interviews, but she had not received any offers. After our time together, she interviewed successfully for a job that she really wanted, and she wrote to thank me:

> Although I was confident that I had the knowledge, skills, and experience required for a position as senior attorney in the law department of a major corporation, your suggestions were very helpful. Particularly helpful was your suggestion to visualize the interviewer wearing a T-shirt beneath his suit jacket with the question "What will you do for *me*?" It certainly ensured that I answered each question and comment with a benefit.

Of course, an interviewer is interested in what you did in your previous job. He is interested in your skills, experience, and education. These are your features, and they are important. However, all things being equal, the candidate who can express the benefits of each feature is the one who will get the job. When you complete every statement with a benefit, the interviewer will see exactly how you can be an asset, and you will increase your chances of success dramatically.

Practice this skill until it becomes a habit. Then, the next time you go for an interview, you too will picture one of your signs on the interviewer's chest: "What will you do for *me*?" And you will be on your way to getting the job you really want.

Features don't change, but benefits can and do, depending on the listener. In Chapter 2 we will learn how to determine which benefits are important to the interviewer and how you can take your features (i.e., skills and experience) and apply various benefits depending on the type of company, the job in question, and the position and needs of the interviewer.

RATE YOURSELF

To determine whether you are ready to move on to the next chapter, ask yourself the questions in Exhibit 1-4, and rate yourself on each one using a scale of 1 to 10.

Exhibit 1-4 RATE YOURSELF: HOW WELL ARE YOU
TRANSLATING YOUR FEATURES INTO
BENEFITS?

	Rating (1–10)
• Am I committed to making a change?	_____
• Do I understand the skill of using features and benefits?	_____
• Am I practicing this new skill daily?	_____
• Have I practiced using my new skill with others?	_____
• Am I making it a habit?	_____

If your self-rating for each of the questions in Exhibit 1-4 is at least 7, forge ahead. However, if you are still struggling, review this chapter and take some more time to practice your new skill before moving on to Chapter 2.

Addressing Each Interviewer's Individual Needs

*When I am getting ready to reason
with a man, I spend one-third of my time
thinking about myself and what I am going
to say and two-thirds thinking about him
and what he is going to say.*

—Abraham Lincoln

Beauty, as they say, is in the eye of the beholder. The same holds true for benefits. Any given feature may offer one benefit to one person and a completely different benefit to someone else. Understanding this concept is essential for effective communication—and for using your feature/benefit skills to their fullest potential during an interview. In this chapter we will learn why the same features offer different benefits to different people.

For example, consider three of the primary participants in a baseball game: the batter, the catcher, and the umpire. The batter has just hit a home run with the bases loaded—a grand slam. The catcher and umpire are watching. All three people are seeing the same situation, but you can be sure they each have different feelings about it:

❑ The batter feels great because his team has earned four runs.

❑ The catcher feels bad because his team just gave up four runs.

❑ The umpire feels indifferent because he does not care who is ahead or behind; his job is simply to judge what happens at the plate.

This single event elicits three different feelings from three different people. In other words, the same thing means different things to different people.

Here's another example: Picture a single red rose. Throughout history, people have endowed flowers with meaning. Certain colors or types have been used to send messages of love, jealousy, friendship, war, and mourning, and have held countless other connections. The meanings attributed to each flower vary from culture to culture and have changed over time. To get an idea of how meaning changes from person to person, let's look at our red rose from nine different points of view—see Exhibit 2-1.

Exhibit 2-1 A SINGLE RED ROSE MEANS DIFFERENT THINGS TO DIFFERENT PEOPLE.

OPTIMIST
It's love and passion.

PESSIMIST
It's thorns and allergies.

REALIST

It's a flower.

IDEALIST

Everyone deserves flowers.

FLORIST

$3.50 each

$35/dozen

SKU No. 221

ENVIRONMENTALIST

We must plant more flowers to stave off global warming.

DRAMATIST

"That which we call a rose

By any other name would smell as sweet."

CAPITALIST

40% markup

BOTANIST

Kingdom—Plantae

Subkingdom—Tracheobionta

Superdivision—Spermatophyta

Division—Magnoliophyta

Class—Magnoliopsida

Subclass—Rosidae

Order—Rosales

Family—Rosaceae

Genus—Rosa L.

Cultivar—Rosa "Grand Prix"

Obviously, not even a simple rose means the same thing to everyone. Now let's look at several examples of how different perceptions and expectations affect communication.

FINDING COMMON GROUND
WITH EACH INTERVIEWER

If you talk with a group of people about dogs, each person will think of his or her own dog or a dog he or she knows. There is no meeting of the minds. Big dog owners will think big; people with small dogs will think small. Even when talking about specific breeds—for example, poodles—some people will think small—toy poodles—and others will think large—standard poodles. To complicate things further, some people *like* dogs and will have warm, pleasant thoughts about them, whereas others may be afraid of dogs or not like them at all, so they will have negative associations. A discussion about your giant dog Brutus may have no relevance to a Chihuahua owner or a cat lover.

Therefore, to improve communication in this example, you would need to tell your listeners what *type* of dog you are talking about and whether you feel positive or negative about it. Then your reference points will make sense to them.

In other words, *features* do not change—a dog is either a Chihuahua or it isn't—but the related *benefits* likely will change depending on the situation. A single feature can have many benefits, and these different benefits will have different values for different people. In our canine example, Brutus is a big dog; that is a feature. But that single feature can have different benefits depending on the listener. Exhibit 2-2 illustrates how one feature (big dog) can have different benefits (or meanings) to different listeners.

Exhibit 2-2 ONE FEATURE HAS DIFFERENT BENEFITS
TO DIFFERENT PEOPLE

FEATURE	LISTENER	BENEFIT
Big dog	Single woman	Sense of protection
	Family	Friendly companion
	Hyper/overachiever	Calming presence

Now let's return to our example of the vacuum cleaner hose from Chapter 1. The *feature* of this particular hose is that "it stretches to twice its normal length." For an employee of a cleaning service, the *benefit* we offered in our example is a perfect fit:

> "The hose on this vacuum cleaner stretches to twice its normal length, so you won't have to bend down as often to plug it in and unplug it. This will make your job easier and faster and will save your aching back."

Now let's say we are talking with the *owner* of the cleaning service. The feature stays the same—the hose still stretches to twice its normal length—but because the owner is not the one who has to bend down continually to plug it in and to unplug it, that benefit would be meaningless to her. However, the same feature of an extendable hose could offer a different benefit to the cleaning service owner:

> "The hose on this vacuum cleaner stretches to twice its normal length, which will save you money and make your people happier and more efficient, lowering your turnover rate."

Note that the feature doesn't change; only the benefit changes.

In Exhibit 2-3, the exercise will help you to begin to develop the skill of finding different benefits for the same feature. In this exercise, think about a restaurant with a large menu of diverse offerings. While concentrating on this one feature—a large, diverse menu—think of an appropriate benefit for each of the potential customers listed. The first one has been completed for you as an example.

Exhibit 2-3 DEVELOPING DIFFERENT BENEFIT
STATEMENTS FOR THE SAME FEATURE

Customer	Feature: Large, diverse menu
	BENEFIT
Mom with four kids	*We have something to make everyone happy.*
Local businessperson	
Out-of-town executive	
Long-haul truck driver	

How did you do? It's easy to see that a large menu might make life a little easier for a mom with four kids: It's hard to please a lot of kids, so the more choices, the better. Here are some possible benefits that might be appropriate for the other customers:

❏ *Local businessperson:* "You can come back every day for lunch and always have something different."

❏ *Out-of-town executive:* "We offer a variety of healthy meal options to keep you healthy during your travels."

❏ *Long-haul truck driver:* "No matter what hours you work, you can have breakfast any time."

Remember, if your sample benefits differ from the ones offered, that doesn't mean they are wrong. Just be sure that you have stated a benefit, not another feature.

UNDERSTANDING THAT MANY FEATURES HAVE MULTIPLE BENEFITS

It gets a little more complicated when there are a number of features, each with a variety of possible benefits. Let's say that you are interested in joining a fitness center. The manager tells you that the health club has 100 machines. That's a feature. What does it do for you? What is the benefit? There is more than one possibility:

❏ You do not have to waste your valuable time waiting to use a machine.

❏ You can exercise next to a friend and keep each other motivated.

❏ The club has a variety of machines to meet all your important exercise needs.

Next, the manager tells you, "Our health club has an indoor track." This is another feature. The possible benefits include:

❑ You can run here in comfort during cold or rainy weather.

❑ You can run on a softer, more even surface, which has less impact on your joints and back, making your run a healthier experience.

❑ You won't have to run in the streets. You can run in safety without having to stop at corners to check for traffic.

DETERMINE WHICH BENEFITS MATTER

You can see that any given feature can have many benefits. The key is to find out which benefits are important to *each person you are talking to*—and when job hunting, this means each person who is interviewing you. Asking questions is important to discovering a person's wants and needs. In the fitness center example just mentioned, before reading off a laundry list of the club's features, a smart club manager would say something like, "You must have a lot of questions for me"— and then would pause and listen. This statement—"You must have a lot of questions for me"—is so simple, but it would make the customer feel important and could elicit a great deal of information that would allow the manager to provide appropriate benefits that are meaningful to *that particular* customer.

To elicit more specific information, the manager could ask, "How do you spend most of your time at a health club?" The answer will allow the manager to customize the benefits for the potential client. For example, if the customer were only interested in using the machines, the manager would just distract and confuse the customer if he concentrated on the benefits of an indoor track. We will discuss how you can learn what is important to an interviewer in later chapters.

ADJUSTING BENEFITS TO SUIT EACH SITUATION

Job hunters who are unskilled in translating features into benefits often make the mistake of using the *same* benefits in every situation and with every interviewer. Remember, the feature stays the same, but it will mean different things to different people. It is up to *you* to determine the appropriate benefit.

Here is a simplified example. In this scenario, you are the owner of a men's clothing store, and the only suits you have left are navy blue with vertical stripes. A man about 4 feet, 10 inches tall walks into your store. What benefit could you offer him for buying your suit? "It will make you look taller," you could tell your "vertically challenged" customer, who probably will recognize that as a benefit, and you will have made a sale.

Later, a man about 6 feet, 10 inches tall comes in looking for a suit. What is the benefit of vertical stripes to him? If you give him the same benefit ("It will make you look taller"), chances are he won't buy the suit because he clearly does not need or want to look taller. In fact, how tall or short the suit makes him look may be completely irrelevant to him. The benefit for *him* may be, "This suit is stylish and makes you look successful."

Unfortunately, in too many cases people use the same benefit over and over, and then they wonder why they don't make progress in their job search. Even when you end your statement with a benefit, if you fail to change the benefit to fit the needs of your listener, you actually could create a *negative* impression. In the first scenario, if the salesperson does not change the benefit to accommodate the tall gentleman's needs, that customer will not buy that suit and most likely will not listen to anything more the salesperson has to say. This is the real danger of applying an inappropriate benefit during an interview. For example, you might think that it's a benefit to *everyone* if you say something like, "I follow directions really well. Just tell me what you want me to do, and I'll do it." Many managers, however, don't want to have to tell you what to do. Instead, they want to hire people who know what their responsibilities are and just do the job, without needing specific directions. Thus the feature of "following directions well" is not a benefit to every interviewer.

Moreover, once you have lost your listener by emphasizing a meaningless benefit, it is nearly impossible to regain his attention. Learning to talk in terms of benefits is not simple. It takes lots of practice and dedication before it comes naturally to you.

Successful politicians live and breathe the skill of adjusting benefits to suit the audience. When campaigning in a mining town, a savvy politician will emphasize one benefit, and when campaigning in an ocean-front town, he will emphasize a completely different benefit. It's not a matter of being all things to all people. Instead, it's a matter of choosing the information that is important to each listener.

Good parents are also experts at using the feature/benefit skill:

❏ "Put your helmet on when you ride your bike so that you won't hurt yourself."

❏ "If you finish your homework now, we can go to the movies later."

❏ "Eat your vegetables so that you can have dessert."

Parents also become skilled at adjusting the benefits to suit the needs of their ever-changing audience. What would be perceived as a benefit by a two-year-old is certainly different from what would be perceived as a benefit by a teenager.

Even within a single age group—let's say teenagers—the benefits will be different for different members. A parent might encourage her child to "study hard" and follow up with a benefit that is meaningful for the particular child:

- ❏ ". . . so that you can get into a good college."

- ❏ ". . . so that you can improve your grades."

- ❏ ". . . so that you can get a good job and earn money for a car."

- ❏ ". . . so that I won't ground you for the rest of your life."

Almost everything parents tell their children ends in a benefit. Effective parents constantly judge the different needs and wants of their children, and they adjust the benefits associated with their statements accordingly.

Exhibit 2-4 will help you to learn how features and benefits relate to specific needs and wants. In this example about a passenger car, the car's features are listed on the left side of the table; possible benefit categories are listed on the right. Each benefit addresses a need or want of a potential customer: comfort, prestige, safety, economy, or convenience. Identify the need or want that each feature/benefit combination addresses, keeping in mind that some benefits may address more than one need or want.

Exhibit 2-4 is not an exhaustive list of possible benefit statements. It is simply an opportunity for you to begin to learn to connect appropriate benefits to a specific need or want and to relate them to a corresponding feature. You may think of other benefit statements that fit our example; that's great. The more you practice, the easier it will be to use this skill during an interview.

Exhibit 2-4 WORKSHEET: RELATING FEATURES AND
　　　　　　　BENEFITS TO SPECIFIC WANTS AND NEEDS

In this exercise, each benefit addresses a need or want of a
potential customer:

1. Comfort　　　　**4.** Economy
2. Prestige　　　　**5.** Convenience
3. Safety

Identify the need/want that each feature/benefit combination
addresses by placing the corresponding number in the blank
space to the right. Keep in mind that some benefits may
address more than one need or want. (The first one has been
completed for you.)

FEATURES	BENEFITS	
GPS system (Global Positioning Satellite)	Shows that you are up on the latest technology.	2
	Will get you where you are going promptly.	
	Will keep you from getting distracted when looking for an exit.	
	Will keep you from getting lost in unfamiliar areas.	
	Keeps you from getting lost and backtracking, thereby saving fuel and money.	
	You won't waste time stopping to ask directions.	
Sun roof	Allows you to enjoy the fresh air and sunshine.	

	Shows your free and independent spirit.	
Large trunk	Allows you to pack a lot for extended trips.	
	Allows you to transport all your goods in one trip, thereby saving gas.	
	Allows you to transport large, awkward objects easily.	
Heated seats	Will make your driving more comfortable in the coldest weather.	
	Will impress your guests by keeping them warm and comfortable.	
	Will keep you warm so that you don't have to wear bulky outerwear to formal occasions.	
Four-wheel drive	Will make your travel smoother on all types of roads in all types of weather.	
	Will help you to handle your vehicle safely in all conditions.	
Cruise control	Keeps you moving at a consistent speed, minimizing fuel consumption.	
	Will help you to relax on long highway drives.	
	Will help you to avoid exceeding the speed limit and getting an expensive fine.	

Now check your answers from Exhibit 2-4 against Exhibit 2-5.

Exhibit 2-5 HOW FEATURES AND BENEFITS REVEAL CUSTOMERS' NEEDS AND WANTS

FEATURES	BENEFITS	NEED/WANT
GPS system (Global Positioning Satellite)	Shows that you are up on the latest technology.	Prestige
	Will get you where you are going promptly.	Comfort, convenience
	Will keep you from getting distracted when looking for an exit.	Safety
	Will keep you from getting lost in unfamiliar areas.	Safety
	Keeps you from getting lost and backtracking, thereby saving fuel and money.	Economy
	You won't waste time stopping to ask directions.	Convenience
Sun roof	Allows you to enjoy the fresh air and sunshine.	Comfort
	Shows your free and independent spirit.	Prestige
Large trunk	Allows you to pack a lot for extended trips.	Comfort
	Allows you to transport all your goods in one trip, thereby saving gas.	Economy

	Allows you to transport large, awkward objects easily.	**Convenience**
Heated seats	Will make your driving more comfortable in the coldest weather.	**Comfort**
	Will impress your guests by keeping them warm and comfortable.	**Prestige**
	Will keep you warm so that you don't have to wear bulky outerwear to formal occasions.	**Convenience**
Four-wheel drive	Will make your travel smoother on all types of roads in all types of weather.	**Comfort**
	Will help you to handle your vehicle safely in all conditions.	**Safety**
Cruise control	Keeps you moving at a consistent speed, minimizing fuel consumption.	**Economy**
	Will help you to relax on long highway drives.	**Comfort**
	Will help you to avoid exceeding the speed limit and getting an expensive fine.	**Safety, economy**

HOW TO SELL YOURSELF BETTER

How you say something can be just as important as *what* you say. For example, at a local farmer's market near my home, there were two vendors selling blueberries. Both had pints and pints of blueberries and a sign. One said "Blueberries," and the other said "Sweet Blueberries." Within half an hour of opening his stall, the vendor with the "Sweet Blueberries" sign had sold out. The vendor with the "Blueberries" sign still had pints left over at the close of the market. Although the berries may have been equally sweet, one of the signs was certainly sweeter.

Here's another example. Look at the signs in Exhibit 2-6.

Exhibit 2-6 WHICH SIGN IS MORE EFFECTIVE?

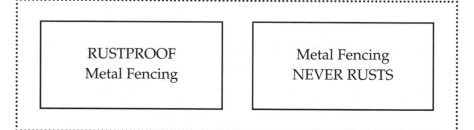

RUSTPROOF
Metal Fencing

Metal Fencing
NEVER RUSTS

At first glance, the signs are virtually the same: Both advertise metal fencing. But these two signs are not the same at all. In the first sign, we are told about a *feature*: "This fencing is rustproof." In the second sign, we see the *benefit*: "This metal fencing never rusts." It is a subtle but distinct difference. Like the "Sweet Blueberries" sign, the "Never Rusts" sign has an *additional* implied meaning. It is saying that this fencing is better—that it will mean less work or will last longer.

Most of us have experienced the frustration of a long delay in a doctor's waiting room. When a patient has waited an hour or more past her scheduled appointment time, it would be only natural to complain to the receptionist. Here is a typical response: "I'm sorry, ma'am, but you can see we are very busy." Would this make you feel less frustrated or upset? Probably not. A feature/benefit approach might save the day in this situation, or at least ease the tension: "Thank you for your patience, ma'am. The doctor was called to an emergency. Rest assured that if you or one of your loved ones were ever involved in a medical emergency, you could count on the same attention and dedication."

What does this mean for you as a job hunter? It means that you must be careful whenever and however you communicate. It's important to know as much as possible about the thoughts, feelings, and views of your listeners to have productive communication. It is particularly important to understand the thoughts, feelings, and views of the *interviewer*.

You must constantly be attuned to your audience whenever you communicate. The same principles apply whether you're talking face to face or over the phone or when you're writing a letter or sending an e-mail. In fact, how you communicate in writing, especially via e-mail, can be even more critical than in face-to-face conversations. In person, you have facial expressions and body language to help you interpret how you are being perceived. In writing, these advantages do not exist.

You should start using your feature/benefit skills beginning with your very first contact with a company for which you are interested in working. Whether you are responding to a help-wanted ad or an online job posting or following up on a tip, your cover letter should take a few of your most important experiences and interpret them as *benefits* for your reader. Offering relevant benefits is essential in this early stage of the process because your first impression will either get or lose you the interview.

CALL ATTENTION TO YOUR FEATURES AND BENEFITS

Before you send out a single résumé, you need to know who you are and what you have to offer. What are *your* features and benefits?

During a job search, you may interview with more than one person within a company: the human resources representative, a potential coworker, the immediate supervisor for the job in question, as well as that supervisor's boss. The *features* of your work experience, skills, and background will not change during these separate interviews, but each of these individuals will have *different needs* and therefore will respond to *different benefits*. It is your task to determine those needs and address them with an appropriate benefit. You must learn to think, act, and talk in terms of what is important to the interviewer.

This means that you need to practice your own set of features and benefits so that they flow smoothly during an interview. You should review every aspect of your résumé, your skills and experience, and develop a variety of benefits for each one. Don't feel that you have to memorize your answers. This will make you seem stilted and uncomfortable. It is more a matter of becoming so familiar with everything you have to offer that you can choose the benefit to suit the needs of the interviewer.

You may ask, "How do I know what is important to the interviewer?"

The first step is *awareness*. Let's take a simple test about interviewers' needs—see Exhibit 2-7. Stop now and check the needs that you believe may be important to a potential interviewer.

If you checked all the boxes in Exhibit 2-7, then you have a new awareness that every interviewer has basic needs that

Exhibit 2-7 WORKSHEET: WHAT ARE THE SPECIFIC NEEDS OF EACH PERSON INTERVIEWING YOU?

☐ The need to please his or her boss.

☐ The need to make the right decision.

☐ The need for an orderly transition.

☐ The need to be perceived as successful.

☐ The need to feel important.

☐ The need to be recognized or remembered.

☐ The need for respect.

☐ The need to accomplish the task at hand in a timely manner.

☐ The need to feel comfortable with you.

most job candidates never even consider. You haven't even met the interviewer yet, and you already know some of his or her needs and wants. As you practice your feature/benefit skills in the worksheet provided at the end of this chapter (in Exhibit 2-10), keep these basic needs and wants in mind.

This new awareness you have about how different people have different needs and desires will help you to uncover their views, feelings, and opinions to a much greater degree. You will learn to be alert to generalities and to ask for clarification when necessary. Chapters 3 and 4 will reveal how honing your listening skills and asking "soft" questions can provide insight into your interviewer that will help you to respond with suitable benefits—and therefore will help to get you the job you want.

What else do employers want? In addition to job-related specifics, employers look for a variety of universal qualities in a candidate. Although these are generalities and will vary from industry to industry and job to job, these qualities usually include:

❑ Job aptitude

❑ Fit with company culture and environment

❑ Ability to get along with others

❑ Willingness to learn

❑ Flexibility

❑ Reliability

❑ Growth potential

❑ Compensation requirements

Knowing what potential employers need, let's look at a nurse who is interested in changing careers to a job in public relations. People skills are a vital part of a successful nursing career and can be translated easily to the public relations field, but the benefits of this singular skill need to be shaped to meet each individual interviewer's needs. Let's look at some of the basic needs listed above and see how our nurse could provide a matching benefit:

1. *Employer's need:* Ability to get along with others.
   Employee's matching benefit: "My experience working with people in pain, as well as the doctors in charge, has taught me how to connect with people in even the most stressful situations. These same skills will allow me to work with

the team under tight deadlines to achieve a successful outcome."

2. *Employer's need:* Fit with company culture and environment. *Employee's matching benefit:* "As a nurse, I worked day, night, and weekend shifts. Each shift had a different feel, with different personnel and different responsibilities. I am able to assess the changing and variable needs of a work environment and adjust quickly to become a productive team member."

3. *Employer's need:* Willingness to learn.
Employee's matching benefit: "Each doctor, nurse, paraprofessional, patient, and family brought different needs and skills to every different situation. I developed the ability to ask pertinent, open-ended questions and listen carefully to the answers to learn as much as possible about each situation and how to approach it. I bring a passion for learning that will make me successful in determining the needs of your clients and translating those needs into vital public relations programs."

Armed with these general wants and needs of the average employer, our candidate was able to change the benefit of her people skills to address three of those requirements with specifics from her past career.

Now try to chart your own set of features and benefits using the worksheet provided. The sample in Exhibit 2-8, based on a fictitious employee, will give you an idea of how to use the worksheet in Exhibit 2-9.

In this simplified example, you can see some real-life features translated into a variety of benefits. In each case, the features and benefits can be combined seamlessly into an effective single statement:

Exhibit 2-8 SAMPLE JOB APPLICANT'S FEATURES/BENEFITS WORKSHEET

FEATURE	BENEFITS			
	Reliability	Expertise	Communication Skills	Leadership Skills
Supervised four employees	Being readily available to help employees.	Sharing extensive knowledge of products/procedures so that team can succeed.	Explaining directions simply and clearly to ensure that employees understand what is expected.	Motivating them to want to succeed.
Increased production 10 percent annually for four consecutive years		By encouraging my staff to increase their own knowledge base, improving the team as a whole.	By rewarding with praise to encourage extra effort.	By regularly reviewing systems to eliminate waste.
Developed training manual	So that staff will understand what is expected and that my expectations are consistent for everyone.	Giving step-by-step directions for every system to get new team members up to speed quickly.	Codifying department policies to ensure consistency.	To improve productivity.

Exhibit 2-9 CHART YOUR OWN EMPLOYMENT FEATURES AND BENEFITS FOR
EACH JOB INTERVIEW

FEATURE	BENEFITS			

❏ "I supervised four employees, explaining directions simply and clearly to ensure that each understood what was expected."

❏ "I increased production by 10 percent for four consecutive years by reviewing all systems on a regular basis to eliminate waste."

❏ "I developed a training manual so that my staff understood what was expected and so that those expectations would be consistent for everyone."

Now use the blank worksheet in Exhibit 2-9 to begin exploring some of your own experiences and skills in terms of features and benefits. Use your résumé to identify your features. Remember, each feature may have many benefits. For each feature you list, try to identify at least two different benefits. You may want to make several copies of this worksheet for practice. Once you have set up an interview, complete a new worksheet, targeting the benefits to address any specifics you have learned about the job or company through your research.

RATE YOURSELF

To determine whether you are ready to move on to Chapter 3, ask yourself the questions in Exhibit 2-10, and rate yourself on each one using a scale of 1 to 10.

If the self-rating for each of these questions is at least 7, move on to Chapter 3. If you are still struggling, though, review this chapter, and take some more time to practice your new skill. This is critical because to ensure that you apply your newly acquired feature/benefit skills effectively, you

Exhibit 2-10 RATE YOURSELF: HOW WELL ARE YOU
ADDRESSING EACH INTERVIEWER'S
INDIVIDUAL NEEDS?

Rating (1–10)

• Do I understand that features do not change? _____

• Do I understand that the same things mean _____
different things to different people?

• Do I understand that benefits change _____
according to what is important to the listener?

• Have I practiced ending each statement with _____
an appropriate benefit?

• Have I analyzed my own skills (features) and _____
thought of a variety of related benefits?

cannot assume anything. You must determine what is important to *each person who is interviewing you,* and the only way to do that is by sharpening your listening skills, learning how to ask questions, and doing your research. The next two chapters are devoted to helping you to understand, develop, and apply these vital tools.

....

CHAPTER 3

Listen Better to Learn What's Important to Each Interviewer

No-one ever listened themselves out of a job.

—Calvin Coolidge,
30TH PRESIDENT OF THE UNITED STATES,
1872–1933

M any people struggle to be good listeners. In school, we are taught how to speak well, read, and write, but no one teaches us how to listen. Yet listening is a vital part of the communication process. And it is absolutely *key* to successful interviewing.

IT'S NOT ABOUT YOU

I can already hear you say, "But wait. Isn't the interview all about *me*? Aren't I the one who should be doing most of the talking? Doesn't the interviewer want to hear about me?"

If you still think that this is true, go back and review Chapter 1. Remember, the only thing the interviewer really wants to know is what you can do for him or her. But how do you know what the interviewer wants? How can you learn what is important to each interviewer? How can you express your skills and experience as a benefit to the interviewer? By *listening*.

Although this seems simple enough, it may not be so easy to figure out how to get the information you need in a traditional interview. Most interviews are set up in a question-and-answer format. The interviewer asks the questions, and the candidate answers them. Under these circumstances, it may seem that you, as the candidate, have no control over the flow of the interview.

Before I launch into how improving your listening skills can give you control and confidence, I'm going to let you in on a little secret: Most interviewers are given little or no training on how to conduct an interview. Often a manager is put in the position of conducting an interview based on the size of the company, growth of the department, position and level of the employee, and a variety of other factors. Some may interview monthly, whereas others may have to interview only once or twice a year. No matter how much experience an interviewer has, it's important to remember that most people hire by their gut feeling.

First impressions are lasting impressions. The interviewer may be every bit as uncomfortable as you are. After all, the interviewer's success depends on making good hiring decisions, and there is usually a great deal of pressure to hire the right person. Bad hiring decisions result in turnovers, and the cost of a turnover is high—often upward of twice an employee's annual salary—in recruiting fees, training costs, lost time, lost productivity, and severance. In addition to the monetary cost of turnovers, bad hires waste time, lose business, cause embarrassment, and breed negative energy among employees. With little training to help them make these expensive decisions, many interviewers hide behind a battery of questions because they don't know what else to do.

Good interviewers have already figured out how to be good listeners. They have honed their listening skills and developed their questions to get the most information they can about a candidate. They listen with their eyes as well as their ears. They pay attention to body language, pauses, eye contact, and subtle language choices.

It's easy to see why listening is important for the interviewer, but why is it important for you as a job candidate? What do your listening skills have to do with how the interviewer feels about you?

WHAT IS A GOOD LISTENER?

A good listener makes the speaker feel important. A good listener makes a connection with the speaker. That connection produces positive feelings in the speaker about *you*. By giving the interviewer your undivided attention—by really listening—you create an atmosphere of mutual respect and interest. As you listen, the interviewer feels good about himself or herself, feels good about you, and feels good about the process. The goal is to create a rapport so that real communication can begin.

Listening is a major factor in achieving success—especially during an interview. It allows you to discover valuable information about the interviewer and what is important to him or her. When you create a positive listening environment, the interviewer feels good about talking to you, revealing information that you can use to talk about benefits that will meet his or her specific needs.

You should recognize that there are a number of distractions and habits that can make listening difficult:

❏ Feeling like you must talk

❏ The nearly uncontrollable urge to think about what you are going to say *next*—instead of paying attention to what the interviewer is saying *now*

❏ Dwelling on questions that are on your mind

❏ Focusing on the interview environment where you may not feel relaxed

❏ Bad habits that can be distracting, such as nail biting, pencil tapping, finger drumming, etc.

The first and most obvious reason to be a good listener is to know exactly what the interviewer is asking and why. Again, this sounds simple enough, but it might not always be easy to know what is behind an interviewer's question.

Let's look at a real-life example. In almost every interview, the first question posed to a candidate sounds something like: "Tell me about yourself."

If you try to answer the question directly, you probably will ramble on and cover areas that may not be of interest to the interviewer. Chances are that you will be doing nothing more than rehashing your résumé. If, as suggested in many job-hunting guides, you launch into a prepared statement about all your strengths, goals, and achievements, you still may not be addressing the needs of the interviewer. Remember, the interviewer is really asking: "What can you do for *me*?" So, when you're finished with your ramblings, where have you left yourself? Nowhere! You have no idea

❏ How to address the needs and wants of the interviewer

❏ What is important to the interviewer

❏ How the interviewer felt about what you said

❏ What the interviewer is thinking (You have become a talk-ing résumé by not distinguishing yourself from the piece of paper that represents you.)

❏ How to translate your skills and experience into benefits that will be meaningful to the interviewer

At best, you are right back to where you started. At worst, you may have turned off your interviewer completely. All you can do after delivering this kind of "background information" is to wait and see what comes next. It does not matter how well you have expressed yourself if the subject is of no interest to your interviewer.

So let's take a different approach, one that will make you feel more in control of the situation. Jared Sparks, an Ameri-can historian and former president of Harvard University, once said, "When you talk, you repeat what you already know; when you listen, you often learn something." If we only learn when we are listening, then the standard interview opening statement—"Tell me about yourself"—calls for a nonstandard response. Instead of launching into a rambling answer or memorized speech, try something like this: "Ms. Jones, I know your time is valuable. What areas would you like me to concentrate on?"

This puts the ball back in the interviewer's court. Here's another little secret: Human beings love to talk about them-selves, and interviewers are only human. It will be refreshing for the interviewer to have an opportunity to concentrate on things that are important to her. More important, her response will give you a much better idea of what the position entails from her point of view, as well as the challenges and concerns she's facing. Armed with this information, you will be able to talk about your experience (which are *features*), ending with *benefits* that you now know are important to Ms. Jones. This will have taken place within the first five to ten minutes of the interview. You don't get a second chance to make a good first impression.

With one simple question, you have taken control of the interview. By finding out what matters to the interviewer, you can channel your energies and responses to addressing those wants and needs. Chances are that you will be less nervous, more comfortable, and more effective throughout the rest of the interview.

Once you have responded to the interviewer's first concerns with your features, ending with a benefit, pause briefly to see what the interviewer might say next. If she asks a follow-up question, you know how to proceed. If she doesn't, you can ask if you should get more specific or move on to other experiences. At each step, listen carefully to how the interviewer responds. As the discussion progresses, you will continue to uncover the specific needs of the company and the interviewer and be able to respond with benefits that will address those needs.

Keep in mind: The most important component of being a good listener is proper preparation.

BE PREPARED

The interview itself can be an overwhelming experience. How can you remember everything? Preparation is key. As Benjamin Franklin said, "Failure to prepare is preparing to fail."

You must have a good grasp of your material—your features (past job experiences, both generalities and specifics; education; skills; additional training; awards; and professional affiliations)—so that you can easily relate them into benefits deemed important by the interviewer. You will find your features spelled out in your résumé. If you have completed all the exercises in Chapter 2, you should have a good understanding of what your features are and now have the skills to translate them into appropriate benefits. Keep practicing this new skill. It will take time to make it a habit. Each time you update your résumé, practice translating those features into benefits.

You should do your homework before your interview. Learn everything you can about the company and the industry. Visiting the company Web site is always a great place to start. Read trade journals and business papers, and go online to check out other business directories—or even visit your public library to use its reference section and online resources. Also, if possible, visit the company before your interview. Learn the route and how long it will take to get there.

The rule of thumb is to dress one step up from the dress code. For example, if the attire is business casual, men should wear a sport coat and tie; women should wear a business skirt and blouse or dress pants. Although it helps to look like you would fit in, no one ever lost a job by overdressing for an interview. It never hurts to wear a conservative business suit.

Next, you need to know who will be interviewing you. Find out the name of your interviewer (including the spelling and pronunciation) and his or her position. You can perform an Internet search of the interviewer. After all, you can be sure that he or she will be researching you! Find out if this person is the decision maker, or if it is someone in human resources. Do a little networking. If you know someone who works for the company (or who used to work there), make a phone call. Finally, see what you can learn about the job itself. Ask your contact person if it is possible to get a copy of the job description.

All this research will allow you to specifically target the benefits of your own expertise during the interview. Don't flaunt your knowledge, but use it to gain more information about what is important to the interviewer. For example:

> "I noticed in a recent *BusinessWeek* article that this company has been number one in the industry for five years in a row. How do you manage to beat your competition so consistently?"

This lets you demonstrate that you keep up with current industry news, and it offers the interviewer a chance to give you valuable insights into the company culture—and what specifically interests *her*. "That was a great article," she might reply. "We rely on innovation to keep us number one. Our department plays a key role in this area. We develop close relationships with our customers, staying in constant communication so that we can anticipate their needs."

In this scenario, the reference to a *BusinessWeek* article touched off an important response. You now know that customer relations and innovative thinking are valuable both to the company in general and to this interviewer in particular. You now can pull from your own experience to demonstrate how you can provide a specific benefit in this area. For example:

> "I've seen firsthand that regular communication with customers is vital. In my current position, I developed a quick and easy monthly e-mail survey. This allowed my customers to answer at their leisure, instead of putting them on the spot, and it generated a lot of constructive feedback. I know I will be able step right in and bring the same kinds of valuable customer responses to your department."

In addition to giving you insight into appropriate benefits, your advance research will allow you to demonstrate a number of skills and traits that are highly prized in the workplace and frequently difficult to convey during an interview, including:

❏ Interest in the position and the company

❏ Ability to work independently

❏ Willingness to take responsibility

❏ Motivation to figure things out for yourself

BRING NOTES

When you go to an interview, it is okay to have notes. You may never use them, but you will be more confident knowing that they exist and that you can refer to them if necessary. Keep your notes brief. You don't want to be fumbling through a lot of paperwork. A single sheet with bullet points of your major accomplishments and a few pertinent facts about the company or industry are probably all you need. *Write big* so that you can take a quick glance at your notes and then return your attention to the interviewer.

You also may want to jot down a key word or two as you are listening to the interviewer so that you can ask relevant follow-up questions or respond to a specific concern with an appropriate benefit.

Exhibit 3-1 is a list of habits that can hurt your ability to be a good listener. Rate yourself by checking "Often," "Sometimes," or "Never."

In this list of bad listening habits, you want to strive for as many checks as possible in the "Never" category. Although self-assessment is important, we are not always the best judges of our own communications skills. Ask someone you

Exhibit 3-1 LISTENING HABITS RATING SCALE

The following is a list of habits that can hurt your ability to be a good listener. Rate yourself by checking "Often," "Sometimes," or "Never."

	Often	**Sometimes**	**Never**
I interrupt.	____	____	____
I jump to conclusions.	____	____	____
I assume rather than ask for clarification.	____	____	____
I finish other people's sentences.	____	____	____
I make up my mind before I get all the information.	____	____	____
I think of things I want to say.	____	____	____
I fail to make eye contact.	____	____	____
I change the subject to what I want to talk about.	____	____	____
I fidget.	____	____	____
I distract the speaker with annoying behaviors (e.g., finger drumming, pencil tapping, hair twirling).	____	____	____
I look at my watch.	____	____	____

trust to be honest to rate your listening skills using the same scale. Do your evaluations match up? Do you think that you are a better listener than others do?

The listening habits you have in daily life relate directly to your interviewing skills. If you or your objective observer thinks that your listening skills need to be sharpened or developed, *now* is the time to make improvements. In addition to becoming a more successful job hunter, your new-and-improved listening skills will continue to benefit you in your new job and in virtually every area of your life.

Listening is a habit. For most of us, our listening habits are developed haphazardly over the years, without much self-evaluation. The first thing you need to do to become a better listener is to *stop talking*. The simple fact is that you cannot listen when you are talking. If you or your objective observer checked "Often" or "Sometimes" in any area of the listening exercise, then you need practice. Tackle each area one at a time, making a conscious effort to improve on or eliminate that one habit before moving on to the next. Bad habits are amplified during stressful situations, such as an interview. Take the time to eliminate your bad listening habits and improve your good ones.

WATCH FOR NONVERBAL COMMUNICATION, TOO

Not all communication is verbal. Ideas and information can be communicated through gestures, facial expressions, attention level, and a host of other nonverbal cues. Often, these nonverbal cues speak louder than words. When you become a good listener, you become tuned-in to every aspect of communication.

Exhibit 3-2 lists a few dos and don'ts about body language during an interview.

Your listening skills communicate a lot about you. Constant interruptions imply that you don't respect the speaker or consider his or her ideas or feelings to be important. If this is something that you have been told all your life—by teach-

Exhibit 3-2 A FEW DOS AND DON'TS OF BODY
LANGUAGE DURING AN INTERVIEW

Do:

- Dress appropriately

- Smile!

- Nod your head

- Make eye contact

- Listen intensely

- Be still but not stiff

- Lean slightly forward in your chair

- Take a few notes to remind you which benefits to emphasize

Don't:

- Fidget

- Pound your fist

- Roll your eyes

- Frown

- Place your hands on your hips

- Look at your watch

- Wring your hands

- Look at the floor

- Assume a stern facial expression

- Sway

- Tap your foot

- Cross your arms

ers, family, and friends—believe it and work to change it. Listening attentively, giving positive feedback, and reflecting back what you have heard communicates to the speaker that you care about what he or she is saying and, by extension, that you value that person.

Good eye contact is a prerequisite for listening. Although the custom of eye contact differs from culture to culture, in this country it is considered good manners for the listener to maintain eye contact with the speaker. This does not mean a stare down, though. You want to seem attentive, not creepy. Also keep in mind that "you're never fully dressed without a smile!"

There are a number of factors that affect the interviewer's ability to listen to *you*. Keep your distracting behaviors under control. Tapping your foot or a pencil, twirling your hair, or "umming" excessively during your responses can distract an interviewer from your message.

Outside influences also can interfere with the interviewer's ability to listen. Perhaps he receives a phone call right in the middle of your answer to his question about your biggest success. Offer to step out during the call. Once the call has ended, the interviewer probably will invite you to continue. Don't do it. He's not listening and does not remember where you were. If he seems at all distracted, offer him the opportunity to comment on the call: "That sounded important." When it is time to return to your previous conversation, briefly reiterate the topic and what you have already said, and then continue. "You asked about my biggest success. As I mentioned, last year I . . . ."

Listening is reacting. It is *being prepared to react* rather than being prepared with information. Conscious listening is the key to success in every area of our lives—interviewing for a new job, interacting with coworkers and supervisors, and promoting satisfying relationships with friends, mates, parents, and children.

LISTENING BETWEEN THE LINES

What is the person really trying to say? What do they want or need? You need to learn to listen between the lines.

For example, let's say you are having a casual conversation with an acquaintance who states, "I think I am getting a cold." What is your response? Do you launch into a long tirade about your last cold? "Oh, I had a cold last week. It was awful. Sneezing, coughing, fever, every symptom you can imagine. I'm feeling better now, but it is still lingering in my chest, and I still get tired. I ran into Sam earlier, and he looked just terrible . . . ."

Or do you go into attack mode? "Oh, do you think you're contagious? I can't afford to get sick. I have a huge presentation next week. I hate when people go around coughing all over everyone."

Your poor friend is probably getting sicker by the minute just listening to you. Put yourself in the other person's shoes and ask yourself, "How would I feel if this was said to me?" or "How would I feel if I was interrupted?" What would a good listener say? "Oh, that's too bad. What are your symptoms?" Now, how do you think the other person would feel about you? She probably would think that you cared about her, that you were a kind person, and she would have good feelings about you.

These good feelings are important. The better the other person feels about you, the more likely he or she is to share his or her thoughts and feelings with you. Listening creates an atmosphere of mutual trust, understanding, and respect.

Why is this important in an interview situation? Much of the information we need is in the minds of other people, not in a business report or on a company Web site. Good listening allows you to find out valuable information without even asking. It gives you insights into the thoughts and feelings of the interviewer, making it possible for you to tailor your responses to his or her specific needs.

Here's a business example. The interviewer begins to talk to you about a subject that is important to his company. Having done your research, you remember reading something about it on the company's Web site. What is your response? "Yes, I read about that on your Web site and I think . . . ." Would the interviewer be impressed by your knowledge and research? Or would he feel frustrated by not being able to finish his thought, idea, or feeling?

A good listener would encourage the interviewer to continue, nodding occasionally and maintaining comfortable eye contact. The three most important words for you to know as a listener are:

❏ *shh*—Say this to yourself as a reminder that your job is to listen.

❏ *uh-huh*—Like a nod, this encourages the interviewer to continue speaking and shows that you are paying attention.

❏ *oh*—Another version of *uh-huh* that prompts the interviewer to go on with his or her thought.

On the other hand, the three words most likely to stop the flow of information from the interviewer are *I, me,* and *mine.* Again, the more the interviewer talks, the more you learn— about the interviewer, about the job, and about the company.

When the interviewer does finish speaking, you might say, "Wow, you sound like you wrote the words on the company's Web site." The interviewer feels respected, knows that you were really listening, likes your compliment, and gives you credit for having checked out the company's Web site.

CONSCIOUS LISTENING

You must become a conscious listener—someone who listens with a purpose. You need to recognize that conscious listening is a skill that takes practice. The next time you go out to dinner with a group of family or friends, become a conscious listener. Sit back and observe how the conversation works.

❑ Who is a good listener?

❑ What makes that person a good listener?

❑ Who constantly interrupts?

❑ How and when do subjects change?

❑ Is good listening rare or common?

❑ What is actually spoken and what is assumed?

❑ How do people show if they are listening or not listening?

❑ Does someone monopolize the conversation? What do you observe in other people when that happens?

If things are going smoothly, disrupt the conversation with one or more of the negative listening habits from the "Listening Habits Rating Scale" in Exhibit 3-1. Then observe what happens.

❑ What happens to the conversation?

❑ What do you observe in the other participants?

❏ Where do people feel uncomfortable?

❏ When does the conversation stop?

❏ How does it get moving again?

❏ What kinds of transitions interrupt the flow of conversation, and which ones facilitate it?

Make a mental note of effective listening techniques, and practice them until they become a part of your own repertoire.

How do you know if you are being a good listener? One good way is to pay attention to how you react when you are in a situation where you really want to hear something—listening to a concert or a great piece of music, watching your favorite television show, or talking on the phone to a long-lost friend. If you hate being interrupted during any of these circumstances, you can be pretty sure that you have been listening well. What happens during these kinds of situations that make it easier or harder to pay attention?

By becoming a conscious listener, you continue to hone your listening skills. One useful tool is to reflect back on what you have just heard. By repeating what the speaker has just said, you are confirming that you heard it correctly. If not, you allow the speaker the opportunity to clarify his or her meaning. Once you are sure that you understand, you can respond appropriately, using your features/benefits skills to their best advantage. Practice conscious listening every day. Obviously, you can do it wherever you go.

TELEPHONE LISTENING SKILLS

Good phone skills are vital during the job-hunting process. At a minimum, you will use the phone to set appointments, get directions, and pick up general information before an interview. More important, you probably will be asked to participate in a phone interview. The sole purpose of a phone interview is to *weed you out!* Your listening skills during a phone interview will play an important role in getting you over this first hurdle.

There are advantages and disadvantages to phone interviewing. On the plus side, you can be dressed for comfort instead of to impress. You can have your notes, résumé, and notepad arranged to suit you, and no one will be the wiser.

On the other hand, you don't have the advantage of seeing the nonverbal signs that are expressed during an interview. You can't read the interviewer's facial expression or body language. You must rely even more heavily on your listening skills to catch minor changes in voice and manner.

There are a number of things you can do to enhance your phone interview experience. As in other interview circumstances, preparation is key. In addition to the research and other groundwork you would do for a standard interview, you must make special preparations for a phone interview.

❏ Plan to conduct the interview on a landline, if at all possible. Cell phones are notorious for poor connections and dropped calls. If you must use a cell phone, pick a place where you know that you get good reception. Never attempt a phone interview while you are driving. In addition to being unsafe, you will not be able to give the interviewer your undivided attention.

❏ Turn off your call waiting. If you don't know how to do this, contact your phone company.

❏ If you live with someone, be sure that they know that you will be interviewing and that they should not interrupt.

Make arrangements for pets and small children so that they will not become a distraction.

❏ Smile. A smile can be heard over the phone.

❏ Dress for success. Although it's important to be comfortable during a phone interview, a certain amount of physical preparation will help you feel your best.

❏ Have a glass of water and take discrete sips to keep your mouth from getting dry.

❏ Take notes. Jot down your questions so that you can continue to listen without interrupting. Be careful, though, that taking notes does not distract you from listening.

❏ Pause before you answer. Five seconds of dead air is a long time over the phone, but you don't have to jump on the interviewer's last words either. Take a breath, form your response in your mind, and then proceed.

❏ Stay seated. Choose a hard-backed chair that will allow you to sit up straight, not lounge. Although you don't want to be stiff, you *do* want to be "on."

❏ Don't multitask. With the advent of cell phones and cordless phones, we are all in the habit of multitasking while we talk on the phone. Don't do it during the interview. Give the interviewer your full attention. Take notes, but don't doodle. *Listen.*

RECORD YOURSELF

Most people have no idea how they sound or act during day-to-day interactions. An excellent exercise is to record some conversations between you and one or two other people, either with an audio or video recorder. Obviously, a video recording will give you more information on your non-verbal communication skills. Play back the tape, and rate yourself again on the "Listening Habits Rating Scale" in Exhibit 3-1.

This can be an eye-opening experience, revealing behaviors that you never knew about yourself.

❏ Do you encourage others to continue their thoughts?

❏ Do you reflect back what you have heard or ask for clarification?

❏ Do you control your distracting habits?

❏ Do you speak too loudly or softly?

Put yourself in the interviewer's shoes and think about how you would feel if you were listening to you.

I hope that you have developed a lust for listening, recognizing the significance of this important communication skill. Let's review what you have learned in this chapter.

We all have a need to be heard. From infancy, we instinctively cry out to be heard, but listening is a *learned* behavior. When you learn to listen, you give the interviewer the opportunity to express himself or herself, meeting *his* or *her* need to be heard. You also discover what is important to the interviewer (remember, the same things mean different things to different people), allowing you to make your responses beneficial to him or her.

1. You can use information that you have learned from the interviewer and *turn your features into benefits* that are meaningful to him or her.

2. You will become more confident during the interview because you will feel more in control—because you will

be answering questions with information that will show your interviewer how hiring you will benefit him or her.

3. You can ask better questions to get essential information.

This chapter also provided some tips to help you conduct a successful phone interview. The skills you are learning apply to every interview situation: traditional face-to-face interviews, phone interviews, teleconferencing, and interviewing over a meal or drinks. The interviewer still cares about the same things. It all comes down to how you present yourself in terms of benefits to the employer.

Listening is a mind-set, and you must set your mind to listen. It takes awareness and practice to develop good listening skills. Once you have made good listening a habit, you will feel more confident and in control, and you certainly will stand out in the crowd. Chapter 4 shows how to ask questions that will help you to identify and deliver the benefits that will get you the job.

RATE YOURSELF

Before you move on to Chapter 4, ask yourself the questions in Exhibit 3-3, and rate yourself on each one using a scale of 1 to 10. Be honest. No one else ever needs to know these scores.

If your self-rating for each of the questions in Exhibit 3-3 is at least 7, move on to Chapter 4. Continue to practice these skills throughout your daily interactions. Good listening fosters mutual respect and understanding. By working to hone your listening skills, you will enhance your chances of getting the job you want and improve your interpersonal relationships at the same time.

Exhibit 3-3 RATE YOURSELF: HOW WELL DO YOU
LISTEN?

Rating (1–10)

- Am I practicing my listening skills in every
area of my life?   _____

- Am I as conscious about what I hear as
what I want to say?   _____

- Do I listen with the intent to listen?   _____

- Have I improved my score on the "Listening
Habits Rating Scale"?   _____

- Do I understand how being a good listener
benefits me?   _____

- Do I understand that listening skills play
an even more important role during
nontraditional interviews (e.g., over the
phone or during a meal)?   _____

···

CHAPTER 4

Asking Questions with Skill and Finesse

*Successful people ask better questions,
and as a result, they get better answers.*

—Anthony Robbins,
ADVISOR AND MOTIVATIONAL SPEAKER

Now that you know how to listen more effectively and how to turn features into benefits, you need to determine what benefits are important to each interviewer and how to discuss your experience and skills in ways that are meaningful to individual interviewers. After all, asking good questions is as important as giving good answers! There comes a time in every interview when you have to ask questions, either to get specific information or to continue the conversation. Although you almost surely will be asked if you have any questions at the end of the interview, don't wait to be asked. It is important that you ask pertinent questions to show both that you have been paying attention and that you are interested in the job. After all, what interviewer would hire a person who does not ask questions during the interview?

Most books and articles on interviewing give a laundry list of potential questions and attempt to teach you pat answers to use during an interview. This book doesn't do that. Memorizing a long list of questions and answers does not allow you to respond *in the moment* to the specific needs and wants of the interviewer. Relying on someone else's questions will make you sound stilted and awkward or slick and superficial, and attempting to reconfigure a memorized answer to fit a question that has been phrased differently will only add to your anxiety. In all the job-search literature, little is written about *why* you need to ask questions, and even less is written about how to do it effectively without rubbing your interviewer the wrong way.

WHY DO YOU NEED TO ASK GOOD QUESTIONS?

Interviewers are motivated by interesting, stimulating questions, but they should not feel as though they are being cross-examined. Job seekers naturally have many questions, and more will arise during the course of an interview. Some will be to find out the specifics of the position; others will be more general in nature. Asking questions, and doing it effectively, is one of the most important components of the interview.

"Most people think all they are supposed to do is *answer* questions during an interview," says Linda Burtch, managing director at Smith Hanley Associates LLC, a national recruiting firm. "I tell all my candidates that their job is to *ask* questions." When you ask good questions, you show that you know the industry and that you have done your homework. With each question you ask, you hone in on what is important to the interviewer.

Learning to pose appropriate questions in your own words also will help you to feel comfortable and confident and demonstrate that you are a strong, independent individual, not a carbon copy of every other candidate. This chapter examines several skills that will help you to ask questions effectively and encourage communication from your interviewer. The more you learn from the person interviewing you, the better you will be able to turn your features into suitable benefits for that specific job.

What you don't know *can* hurt you. If you launch into a monologue about yourself, you might make unwarranted assumptions about the interviewer, the company, or the position. You may miss what is important to the interviewer and even risk being offensive. Simple things—such as whether you are the first or last interview of the day or of the overall search—can influence how the interviewer perceives you. If you don't ask, you can't know.

THE DIFFERENCE BETWEEN OPEN- AND CLOSED-PROBE QUESTIONS

This is a skill known by most salespeople, and once you know how, you can use it successfully during an interview. *Closed probes* are questions that require a specific answer or clarification. Generally, closed probes limit responses and should be used only if you need a very specific answer.

In contrast, when you use an open probe, you get more than just the facts. You give the other person room to explain, often eliciting a range of value-based information, such as feelings, attitudes, and opinions. When you know how a person feels about the information, you know how to respond with a fitting benefit.

Closed probes can lead to awkward, never-ending conversations that are frustrating to both of you. Let's look at an example. I want to know what kind of ice cream you like. Using a closed probe, I would ask, "Do you like vanilla ice cream?" The answer would be either "Yes" or "No." Then I would have to ask, "Do you like chocolate ice cream?" Obviously, this could go on forever.

An open probe still may give you a specific answer, but it also might give you greater insight into the mind of the other person. Here is our example using an open probe: "What kind of ice cream do you like?" The answer could be, "Well, I love chocolate ice cream, especially chocolate milk shakes, but I haven't had one in three years. I'm watching my calories." Not only do you know that your listener loves chocolate ice cream, but you also know that he is avoiding high-caloric desserts, so you could offer an alternative that would meet his current needs.

As you can see, an open probe generally provides more complete and valuable information than a closed probe. Furthermore, the interviewer tends to feel more comfortable with this style of question, which is less aggressive and more conversational in nature. As mentioned in Chapter 3, most interviewers have little or no training in the interview process, so if you bombard them with a series of direct questions, they may feel defensive or under attack. On the other hand, most people enjoy talking about what they know, and by phrasing questions smoothly using open probes, you enable the interviewer to give expansive answers.

Here is an example specific to job interviewing. Let's say that you want to find out about salary. Some closed probes and their answers might be

Question: "What is the salary for this job?"
Answer: "We are offering x amount per year."

Question: "What are the employee benefits?"
Answer: "We offer a standard benefit package."

In contrast, an open probe would be

> "Could you please discuss compensation?"

With a question such as this, the interviewer is far more likely to go into detail about the entire compensation package. He might respond

> "Well, our starting salary for this position is in the mid $50s but, depending on your performance, we will review your salary in six months and again in a year. We have an excellent benefit package that includes two weeks' vacation and a choice of health plans. I'm also excited to tell you that we are building an on-site health club that should be finished by the end of the year."

This is a lot of information from one well-phrased question. You now know

❑ The starting salary

❑ That the benefits are flexible

❑ That the company continues to build benefits into the work environment

❑ That you can expect the salary for this position to be raised at least once (possibly twice) within the first year

❑ That the interviewer expects you to be a high performer to earn those increases

❑ That physical fitness is important to this interviewer

In this example, a good follow-up question might be

"I'm wondering how is success measured?"

Again, this is an open probe that leaves plenty of room for the interviewer to elaborate on all the ways you might be evaluated, both formally and informally. Notice how these open-ended questions facilitate the conversation and make it easy for the interviewer to provide you with valuable information.

Remember, the more the interviewer talks, the more you learn. The more you learn from the interviewer, the better chance you will have to relate your features to appropriate benefits. When necessary, you can always follow up with closed probes to get specific answers with such questions as

❑ "Can I get into the office early or stay after hours?"

❑ "Is there on-site parking for employees?"

❑ "Is there a cafeteria?"

Keep in mind that these very specific questions are probably more appropriate in a second interview, when you know that the interviewer is definitely interested in you.

Exhibit 4-1 is a quiz to help you recognize the difference between open probes and closed probes.

All the questions in Exhibit 4-1 are closed probes. Here is a simple way to determine whether a probe is open or closed: If it can be answered in one word (often "Yes" or "No") or just a few words, it is a *closed probe.* In contrast, if it includes hints as to *how the interviewer feels* about the subject at hand, it is an *open probe.*

Once you get the hang of it, it is not difficult to ask an open-probe question instead of a closed one. The worksheet in Exhibit 4-2 gives you a chance to try using open probes immediately.

Exhibit 4-1 OPEN-PROBE/CLOSED-PROBE QUIZ

Indicate whether you think that each query is an open or closed probe. Use the letter **O** for an open probe and the letter **C** for a closed probe.

"Did you have a good trip?" _____

"Do you like hot dogs or hamburgers?" _____

"Did you enjoy your vacation?" _____

"Do you like the leather seats in your new car?" _____

"Was your time on jury duty tedious?" _____

"What is the salary for this position?" _____

"When would I be able to get a raise?" _____

"Is this a new position?" _____

"How long have you been in your job?" _____

"When will you be making a hiring decision?" _____

All of the questions above are closed probes. In the following worksheet, practice rewording them as open probes.

Exhibit 4-2 PRACTICE CHANGING CLOSED-PROBE
QUESTIONS INTO OPEN-PROBE QUESTIONS

Write an open-probe question for each of the following closed-probe questions. (The first question is done for you as an example.) Keep in mind that your goal is to elicit as much information as possible. Practice using your own words with this skill, which will help you to feel comfortable and in control.

Closed probe: "Did you have a good trip?"

Open probe: <u>*"How was your trip?"*</u>

Closed probe: "Do you like hot dogs or hamburgers?"

Open probe: _____

Closed probe: "Did you enjoy your vacation?"

Open probe: _____

Closed probe: "Do you like the leather seats in your new car?"

Open probe: _____

Closed probe: "Was your time on jury duty tedious?"

Open probe: _____

Closed probe: "What is the salary for this position?"

Open probe: _____

Closed probe: "When would I be able to get a raise?"

Open probe: _____

Closed probe: "Is this a new position?"

Open probe: _____

Closed probe: "How long have you been in your job?"

Open probe: _____

Closed probe: "When will you be making a hiring decision?"

Open probe: _____

After you've completed Exhibit 4-2, take a look at Exhibit 4-3, which gives some suggestions for how each of these closed-probe questions can be changed to open-probed questions. Compare your answers against these.

Exhibit 4-3 SAMPLE OPEN-PROBE QUESTIONS

1. *Closed probe:* "Did you have a good trip?"

   Open probe: "How was your trip?"

2. *Closed probe:* "Do you like hot dogs or hamburgers?"

   Open probe: "What kinds of food do you like?"

3. *Closed probe:* "Did you enjoy your vacation?"

   Open probe: "Tell me about your vacation."

4. *Closed probe:* "Do you like the leather seats in your new car?"

   Open probe: "How do you like your new car?"

5. *Closed probe:* "Was your time on jury duty tedious?"

   Open probe: "How was jury duty?"

6. *Closed probe:* "What is the salary for this position?"

   Open probe: "Would you please discuss the compensation package?"

7. *Closed probe:* "When would I be able to get a raise?"

   Open probe: "How does the job evaluation process work?"

8. *Closed probe:* "Is this a new position?"

   Open probe: <u>"Will you please explain the structure of</u>
   <u>this department?"</u>

9. *Closed probe:* "How long have you been in your job?"

   Open probe: <u>"You seem like you have been with the</u>
   <u>company for quite a while."</u>

10. *Closed probe:* "When will you be making a hiring decision?"

    Open probe: <u>"How will the decision-making process</u>
    <u>work in terms of hiring for this position?"</u>

This is also an easy skill to practice because it can be used in virtually any situation, from dinner to a discussion about the weather with a complete stranger in an elevator. People who ask open-probe questions are usually good listeners. Pay attention to the conversations around you to see who uses open probes regularly and comfortably, and notice what kinds of responses they get.

SHOW WHAT YOU KNOW

In addition to getting you the information you need, asking the right questions gives you an opportunity to show what you know. How does *asking* a question illustrate your knowledge? It is not necessarily *what* you ask, but *how* you ask it. Before any interview, you should have researched the company, the interviewer, and the position. By framing your question appropriately, you can demonstrate the research you have done, your interest level and enthusiasm, and your ability to think and act independently. Here are just a couple of examples of how you can show your knowledge as you ask a question:

❏ "I read in *Forbes* that the company has increased its profit margin by 25 percent. What do you think are the major factors that have contributed to this remarkable success?"

❏ "I know that your company has experienced dramatic growth over the last three years. What qualities do you look for in a new hire that will help you to continue this growth?"

Posing a well-thought-out question that demonstrates your knowledge and research is a powerful interviewing tool. It can allow you to reveal the depth of your understanding without seeming immodest and to convey a high level of interest in your field without making you seem like a know-it-all. By asking rather than telling, you flatter the interviewer by inviting him or her to share his or her own experience and expertise.

ASKING "SOFT QUESTIONS" TO ELICIT MORE INFORMATION FROM YOUR INTERVIEWER

Another important interview skill is learning how to ask what are known as "soft questions." You may already be familiar with this approach, but if not, in short, it simply means asking questions in a nonabrasive, indirect manner to elicit more meaningful and extensive responses.

As I've mentioned repeatedly, trying to use someone else's words during an interview is uncomfortable. It can make you self-conscious, distracted, and even more nervous. Throughout this book you have been practicing a number of skills that are designed to make you more effective using your own words and your own style. This section examines traditional interview questions and gives specific instructions for developing the skill of using soft questions. The examples presented are not meant to be memorized but to help you develop productive communication techniques. The examples provided will give you an idea of how you can take control of an interview and improve your comfort level—as well as that of your interviewer.

Avoid Asking Abrasive Questions

Almost every book on the topic of interviewing lists a number of questions that in particular you should ask during an interview. Some typical suggestions include

❑ "How would you describe this job?"

❑ "What are you looking for in a candidate for this position?"

❑ "Who will be my supervisor?"

❑ "Can I have a copy of the organizational chart?"

❑ "How did this job opening occur?"

❑ "How long have you been working here?" Or "Do you like working here?"

❑ "What is the next step?"

I classify these examples as *abrasive questions*. And although there is nothing inherently wrong with the *subject* of each of these questions, when you ask them so directly, you can make an interviewer feel like he or she is on a witness stand in a courtroom.

The Benefit of Asking Soft Questions

In contrast, the skill of asking soft questions is a way to help the interviewer feel more comfortable. This, in turn, will encourage more detailed responses, allowing you to get a better understanding of the benefits that are important to the interviewer. For example, a typical question that candidates are encouraged to ask sounds something like, "Tell me about your company." (which isn't really even a question). In response, you are likely to get a litany of statistics that can be found on the company Web site—and if you've done your research before getting to the interview, you should know all these answers.

❑   "We are a Fortune 500 company and a leader in our field."

❑   "We did $20 million in sales last year."

❑   "We build the world's best widgets."

So here is how you might rephrase this into a soft question:

> "I know your company is a leader in the field. What do you think makes it so successful?"

With this type of soft question, you show that you already have some knowledge of the company's position, so the interviewer can skip over the basic statistics and move on to more meaningful information, including his thoughts and feelings about where the company stands. He even may reveal some of his own goals, as well as how he sees you fitting into the picture.

MAKE LEADING STATEMENTS
INSTEAD OF ASKING QUESTIONS

Sometimes a soft question is not a question at all but rather a *leading statement* followed by a significant pause that allows the listener time to respond. When using a leading statement, just as when asking a question, you must leave an opening for the interviewer to reply. Here is an example of how to rephrase a standard interview question in the form of a leading statement:

Standard question: "What do you look for in a candidate?"
Leading statement: "You probably have a sense about the qualities needed for someone to do a great job for you."

As you can see in this example, you are *inviting* the interviewer to give specific examples of what she is looking for in the person who will get the job. This is an ideal way to get the information you need to answer with meaningful benefits that will meet your interviewer's specific wants and needs.

KNOW WHEN TO ASK QUESTIONS

It may be better to ask some questions before an interview or, as mentioned earlier, save some for a second interview. For example, it is not a good idea to ask for a copy of the company's organizational chart during a first interview. Whenever possible, it is best to request this information during your research prior to the interview. Call or e-mail your contact person asking for a copy of the organizational chart, as well as the job description, if available. Having this information ahead of time will help you to prepare for the interview. Asking for it during the interview will make you look ill-prepared, nervous as you fumble with the paper, and inattentive if you try to review it on the spot.

If you are unable to get the information you need prior to the interview, instead of asking for the organizational chart, try using one of the soft questions or leading statement techniques:

> "I'm wondering how this job fits into the overall organization."

This invites the interviewer to give you much more information than you ever will find on an organizational chart or in a written job description. Even if you have seen a job description, you can use these techniques to ask for more detailed information:

> "I think I have a general understanding of what the job entails, but I would like to know if you have any additional information."

EXAMPLES OF SOFT QUESTIONS

Let's take a closer look at another example of a soft question and how it will help you to get the information you want, as well as possibly getting a hint about how the interviewer feels about you.

Standard question: "Where do I stand, and what is the next step?"

Soft question: "Would you please tell me about the hiring process for this position?"

"What is the process?" This is a key phrase that leaves an opening for the interviewer to provide you with a lot of valuable information. The response could answer several more direct questions with specific details:

❑ "What is going to happen?"

❑ "When will I know?"

❑ "Where do I stand?"

❑ "Who is involved in the decision-making process?"

Now take another look at the list of standard interview questions and rephrase them as soft questions *or* as leading statements using Exhibit 4-4.

Exhibit 4-4 PRACTICE ASKING SOFT QUESTIONS AND MAKING LEADING STATEMENTS

Rephrase the following list of standard interview questions by changing them to soft questions or leading statements. Use your own words so that you can become comfortable with the process.

Standard question: "How would you describe this job?"

Soft question or leading statement: _____

_____

Standard question: "Who will be my supervisor?"

Soft question or leading statement: _____

_____

Standard question: "How long have you been working here?" Or "Do you like working here?"

Soft question or leading statement: _____

_____

Standard question: "What are the expectations of the person you hire for this job?"

Soft question or leading statement: _____

_____

SOFT QUESTIONS AND LEADING STATEMENTS

To see how you did in Exhibit 4-4, check your answers against those below. Again, there is no right or wrong answer. Your goal is simply to give subtle encouragement to your interviewer to keep talking and provide more information. As always, don't try to memorize any of these suggestions.

Standard question: "How would you describe this job?"
Leading statement: "I think I have some understanding of the job requirements, but I would appreciate your views."

Standard question: "Who will be my supervisor?"
Soft question: "Will I have the pleasure of working for you?"

Standard question: "How long have you been working here?" Or "Do you like working here?"
Leading statement: "You seem very happy here."

Standard question: "What are the expectations of the person you hire for this job?"

Soft question: "What special qualities do you feel are needed for someone to be successful in this job?"

SIMPLE PROMPTS TO KEEP YOUR INTERVIEWER TALKING

To keep your conversation moving and to encourage your interviewer to provide additional information, you also can use a variety of prompts—subtle words, phrases, or even body language that gently nudge the interviewer. The following prompts, posed in the manner of soft questions, are intended to keep the interviewer talking. Listen carefully for information that you can use later in the interview or in your follow-up thank-you letter.

1. "Oh?" Yes, this really is a soft question that can prompt the interviewer to continue. It's simple but very effective.

2. "You must have lots of questions." This puts the ball back in the interviewer's court. The tenor and tone of the questions that follow and the order in which they are asked will give you clues as to their importance.

3. "That's a good question." When you use this prompt, it is especially important to pause. The goal is to encourage the interviewer to elaborate further before you respond. It can buy you some time and may give you an indication about which benefits you need to express.

4. "I get the feeling that . . . " This prompt is part of a skill set known as *active listening.* It shows that you have been

paying attention by allowing you to reflect back what you have just heard. The interviewer will either confirm your assumption or make a clarification. In either case, you will have a better idea of how to proceed.

5. "Good observation" (then pause). As I have noted, everyone likes a little praise. Coming from you, the candidate, it can be pleasantly surprising. Remember, most people who are interviewing don't do it for a living. Anything you can do to make them feel more comfortable will move you up a notch in their eyes.

6. Nodding. Although this is obviously not a question, it is an important part of active listening and a key way to encourage the interviewer to continue to talk while you learn. Gentle nodding during an explanation shows that you are following the interviewer's line of thought. It is important to maintain eye contact while you are nodding so that you don't seem dismissive or like your mind is racing ahead to what you want to say next.

7. "What makes you say that?" (asked gently with a smile). The smile is key. You do not want to seem defensive. The goal of this prompt is to get clarification about the real meaning behind an interviewer's question or comment. This can be tricky and takes practice.

8. "I think you mean . . . ." Again, this is an active listening response. You are looking for clarification by reflecting back what the interviewer has said, giving him or her a chance to confirm, expand, or clarify the meaning.

Here are just a few more ways you can start an unobtrusive question. Try them out, play with them, and find the phrases that make you feel most comfortable.

❏ "I'm wondering if . . . ."
❏ "Perhaps you could tell me . . . ."
❏ "I'm just curious about . . . ."

Again, it is more important to understand and master the skill of asking unobtrusive questions than to memorize any particular phrase. Your tone and attitude go a long way toward delivering these soft questions effectively. Relax, smile, and ask your question with an attitude that you are genuinely interested in the answer.

WHY THESE SKILLS ARE IMPORTANT

Open probes, soft questions, leading statements, and simple prompts are important skills that take practice. Combined with good listening, they can provide you with clear insight into how to express benefits about your skills and experience that will be meaningful to your interviewer. Even if you don't receive an offer, if you have asked good questions, you will be armed with valuable information and be better prepared for the next interview.

To use these skills effectively, you must make them a habit—and that requires

Practice

Patience

Persistence

More practice

The good news is that you can easily practice these skills with your family and friends. Try it the next time you go out to dinner, and observe the differences in the responses you get. You can gauge your success on how much information you learn, how comfortable your companions are, and how much talking they do. Ideally, here's what should happen:

❏ The more they talk, the more you listen.

❏ The more you listen, the more you learn.

❏ The more you learn, the better your responses.

❏ The better your responses, the more successful the conversation.

If you can use this approach in your day-to-day conversations, you can get it to work in an interview. Remember: *The more you learn, the more you earn.*

At the very end of the interview, once you have asked a variety of compelling questions that demonstrate your interest in the job, your knowledge of the industry, and your ability to provide valuable benefits to the interviewer, you may be asked again if you have any additional questions. At this point, it is fine to say something like, "No, thank you. You have done a great job." Everyone, even an interviewer, likes to hear a compliment now and again, and you end the interview on a positive note.

RATE YOURSELF

Do you have a thorough understanding of how and why to ask questions unobtrusively? Rate yourself on a scale of 1 to 10 using the worksheet in Exhibit 4-5 before you move on to Chapter 5.

If you have given yourself a rating of 7 or above for each of the questions, then you can move on to Chapter 5. If you are still struggling, though, review this chapter and practice, practice, practice.

Exhibit 4-5 RATE YOURSELF: DO YOU KNOW HOW AND
WHY TO ASK QUESTIONS UNOBTRUSIVELY?

Rating (1–10)

- Do I know the difference between closed
  and open probes?   _____

- Do I understand why it is important to
  use open probes during an interview?   _____

- Have I practiced using open probes until I am
  able to use them easily and comfortably?   _____

- Do I understand the meaning of soft
  questions?   _____

- Do I understand why using soft questions
  and leading statements is important
  during an interview?   _____

- Have I practiced rephrasing standard
  questions into soft questions?   _____

- Do I recognize and know how to use simple
  prompts to encourage the interviewer to
  keep talking?   _____

- Have I practiced using these other kinds
  of prompts?   _____

....

CHAPTER 5

Answering Questions with Outstanding Benefits

A slip of the foot you may soon recover,
but a slip of the tongue you may never get over.

—Benjamin Franklin

We have covered how to *ask* questions in an interview, but we all know that the bulk of your time during an interview will be spent *answering* questions. Most interview guides list hundreds of questions and attempt to tell you how to answer all of them. The fact is that it is impossible to anticipate every question that may arise during an interview and create a scripted answer for each one. More important, it is a waste of time and energy.

The interviewer is interested in *you*, not in the answers of some interview "expert"—certainly not *my* answers. *Your* skills, *your* experience, *your* words, and *your* answers are what are important to the interviewer. Regardless of the questions asked, the skills we have already learned are all you really need to know to answer them:

❏ Ending your answers with a benefit important to the interviewer (Chapter 1)

❏ Remembering that the same thing means different things to different people (Chapter 2)

❏ Listening to what is important to the interviewer (Chapter 3)

❏ Asking skillful questions (Chapter 4)

Here is the truth about answering questions in an interview: There is no simple, padded answer that you can memorize that will guarantee you the job. Interviewing is hard work and requires you to use all the skills I've discussed so far with a certain degree of mastery. The skills you have been learning will help you to answer *any* question you are asked. As I've said many times, no one cares about your experience and skills (i.e., the *features* of your work experience) unless you can show how they will make the interviewer happy that he or she hired you (i.e., the *benefits* you will bring to the job). Don't forget—the interviewer is under pressure to make the right hiring decision, so you must make it easy for the interviewer to choose *you*. Be aware that he or she also wants to make *his* or *her* boss happy.

THREE TYPES OF QUESTIONS YOU SHOULD BE PREPARED TO ANSWER IN ANY INTERVIEW

I have found that the majority of interview questions fall into one of three categories:

1. Questions you hate to be asked

2. Standard (i.e., predictable) questions that almost every interviewer asks

3. Questions that mean the interviewer is really interested in you

To practice all the skills you have learned in the context of answering interview questions, I have chosen three sample questions from each area. They may or may not be questions that you will hear in an interview, but they are representative of the *types* of questions that you are likely to encounter. The following examples are meant to help you break down the process and see how to apply each skill to a real interview question.

Do not attempt to memorize the answers; it won't do you any good. Even if the interviewer asks a similar question, the phrasing may be just different enough that the answer I have given will sound stilted at best and ridiculous at worst.

QUESTIONS YOU HATE TO BE ASKED— AND HOW TO ANSWER THEM WELL

Everyone has at least one question he or she dreads. It may be something general that seems too hard to answer without tripping yourself up, or it may be something specific having to do with a bad experience. I say *embrace* the question you most dread. Welcome it! Why? Because every question is an opportunity for you to show how you can benefit the interviewer. Since you cannot choose the questions you will be asked during an interview, you must be prepared to answer anything. When it comes to that most dreaded question, you have only two choices:

❑ You can sweat through the entire interview, hoping against hope that the question won't be asked and fumbling when it finally comes.

or

❑ You can "own" that thing that scares you most, prepare for it, and welcome it as an opportunity to shine where others typically fail.

If you can learn to love the most dreaded question and answer it with poise and confidence, you will sail through any interview. You will feel relaxed and in control—prepared for anything. First, you must determine what your most dreaded question is. This should not be too hard. When you talk about your career, what area do you avoid? What makes you cringe? Take a few minutes to confront that experience honestly.

I have found that many people have trouble with some version of these three questions:

❑ What are your weaknesses?

❑ Tell me about your former boss.

❑ Why were you fired?

Although your personal "most hated" question may be different, let's answer the ones above and perhaps you will learn to welcome your own hated question.

Before we move on, I would like to tell you about the work I have done with past offenders about to be paroled. As part of my consulting business, I have provided pro bono workshops for soon-to-be-released convicts on the art of interviewing. As a condition of their parole, they are expected to look for and find steady employment. Most applications require you to disclose whether you have been convicted of a felony. Lying on a job application is grounds for dismissal and, in some cases, is against the law. Furthermore, such a lie almost certainly will be discovered because most companies today conduct some kind of background check.

I counsel these job seekers to address this question up front, admitting what they have done briefly, but with as much honesty as possible, and stating what they have learned from the experience and how that knowledge will benefit the potential employer.

So the next time you worry about how to answer, "Why were you let go?" or "What is your biggest weakness?" think about these former convicts and what *they* have to face as they enter the job market. Your biggest weakness will look small in comparison. If they can turn jail time into a benefit, you can turn lessons you have learned into a benefit as well.

Executive recruiter Linda Burtch, managing director at Smith Hanley Associates LLC, concurs that it is vital to address tough issues head-on. "If you have an issue in your career—such as a new job every year for the last four years—get your story together," she advises. "Know why it happened and be prepared to explain what you have learned." For example, you might say

> "I have moved around a lot. I had never taken the time to research the company before, and I have learned from that mistake. This time around, I have done my research, and I know I can make a commitment here and do a good job for you."

As we go through answers to my sample questions, think about them in terms of your own most hated question. How have the skills you have learned been applied to the sample answer? How can you use what you have learned to answer *your* most hated question? We are working on developing your *skills* here, not creating padded answers. Let's take our sample questions one at a time.

"What Are Your Weaknesses?"

We all have weaknesses and should learn to recognize them. To prepare yourself to respond to this kind of query during an interview, you need to ask yourself the following questions:

❏ Do you recognize your weaknesses?

❏ What are they?

❏ What have you done about them?

❏ What are you continuing to do about them?

❏ Have they diminished?

Once you have examined your weaknesses, you can concentrate on where you have made improvements and learn to respond to a question about them without going weak in the knees.

Let's say that your weakness is being a poor listener. Perhaps you recognized this weakness several years ago. Once you recognized it, you may have read books on listening, taken seminars, and practiced listening skills with your family, friends, and coworkers. If you have any performance reviews documenting your improvement in this area, be sure to bring copies with you to the interview.

Now, you might admit that although you are still not perfect, you have an improved awareness of what it takes to be a good listener and are now much more proficient. You can mention the benefits of being a good listener at work and how your efforts have improved your performance or contributed to a specific success. Below is a sample answer. Don't try to memorize the words; concentrate on the process, and remember that the process can be applied to anything.

"My major weakness was that I was not a good listener. I found out that I was only thinking of what I wanted to say when someone else was talking. I read two books on how to listen [*Mention them by name*], took a seminar on listening skills, and asked my friends to help me become more conscious of when I was interrupting [*Feature: Developed a new skill*]. This has been an ongoing learning experience. I have shown improvement and have a better understanding of listening being vitally important to be a good manager, getting along with coworkers, and accomplishing company goals [*Benefit: You bring this new skill with you, and it will make you a good leader in this company*]."

"Tell Me about Your Former Boss"

The first thing you should know about answering this question is that it is *never* appropriate to bash a former employer. It is bad form. It makes you look indiscreet, immature, and whiny. It projects a negative image of *you* rather than of your former employer. It also makes people wonder what you would say behind their backs.

Having said that, I just noted that everyone has strengths and weaknesses. It would be disingenuous to make your former employer out to be a saint. This is the time to learn to be a bit of a tightrope walker. Here is a sample response:

"She had many strengths. She worked hard, seemed to know her stuff, and always looked for ways to improve. I would have liked her to give me more specific directions, review my progress during the course of our work, not just at the end of a project, and

have more one-on-one meetings about my performance. We had reviews only once a year. When I get
regular feedback [*Feature: Responds to feedback*], I can
turn it around and implement the changes immediately [*Benefit: Able to implement changes quickly for this
company*]."

In this example, you praise your boss and avoid direct criti-
cism. By explaining that you would have liked more frequent
reviews, you are revealing your work style and showing what
you are looking for in your next position rather than com-
plaining about your former situation. You show that you have
learned more about yourself and have grown from the experience, and you end with a benefit that shows that you will
do a better job.

Some interviewers employ guerilla tactics—deliberately
putting you on the spot to see how you respond under pressure. One example of this approach is to ask a candidate
about his boss's weaknesses. As mentioned, you do not want
to launch into a tirade about how much you hated your former supervisor. Recognize the tactic for what it is—a kind of
test. Stay calm, think about what you have discovered about
what is important to the interviewer, and focus on the benefits. Talk about what you have learned from your supervisor's
mistakes and how that knowledge will benefit your new
employer.

Using the example I gave about a supervisor with poor
communication skills, you can be even more specific about
what lesson you have taken from your supervisor's mistakes:

"I have learned how regular feedback is important
to an employee's success, and I will be sure to follow
up with both my supervisor and my direct reports so
that we can address any problems as they arise."

"Why Were You Fired
(or Laid Off or Downsized)?"

There may be perfectly legitimate reasons for losing a job that have little or nothing to do with your job performance: The company is downsizing, the company merged with another company and laid off people whose positions were duplicated, or a new boss brings in his or her own team. No matter what the reason, if you were asked to leave a job, there will always be questions—Why you and not the other person?

You need to know how to answer these questions directly, honestly, and without becoming defensive. If you were fired for cause, acknowledge the reason, and speak about what you have learned and what you have done to correct the situation. This newly acquired knowledge will make you a valuable employee. The following are three examples for responding to the question "Why were you let go?"

1. *Required relocation:* "It's true that I was let go. My company merged with XYZ Corporation, which is headquartered in Orlando, and the company wanted me to relocate. I was concerned that the merger had unsettled the company to the point where it could not guarantee my job even if I did relocate, and I decided not to move my family under the circumstances. Basically, I did not see any growth opportunity. I am flattered, however, that the company thought enough of my contributions to offer to spend thousands of dollars to relocate me. It shows that the company did appreciate my hard work, dedication, and relations with customers and my coworkers [*features*]. I will bring this same dedication to work for you [*benefit*]."

2. *Boss brought in his own team:* "I was fired because my new boss brought in one of his past employees. Our job

descriptions were similar, and his loyalty was to the person he brought into the company. My most recent annual reviews show that I worked hard and always got things done properly and on time [*Feature: Hard worker with good time management skills*]. I can bring my time management skills to work for you [*benefit*]."

3. *Fired for cause:* "This was the first job I ever had as a supervisor. Until that time, I had been responsible only for the work I was assigned. Suddenly, I was in the position of supervising two other employees, making assignments, and evaluating their work. I was ill-prepared and did not know how to delegate. I tried to do everything myself, our team missed several deadlines, and I was held accountable for the loss of business.

   "I can honestly say that being fired has been the best thing that could have happened to me. I realized that I needed to develop my management skills [*Feature: Recognizes need for change*]. I took three courses in business management at the local community college and read several current books on management. I have come to realize that my past successes happened in *spite* of my weakness. I have volunteered at the local Y, and I asked to run their counselor-in-training program. I was responsible for recruiting and training a team of eight volunteers. It allowed me to practice the new management skills I had learned in a real-life situation and learn to delegate. As I continue to improve my supervisory skills, I will bring more productivity and accountability to the job and be an even better worker for my new employer [*benefit*]."

Exhibit 5-1 is a simple worksheet that nevertheless can help you to think about how you can turn *your* weaknesses into benefits.

Exhibit 5-1 HOW TO MAKE A WEAKNESS INTO A BENEFIT

List at least three questions you hate to be asked in an interview:

1. _____

   _____

2. _____

   _____

3. _____

   _____

Briefly explain what worries you most about each question:

1. _____

   _____

2. _____

   _____

3. _____

   _____

Now, explain what you have done to make improvements and what you have learned. Keep your answers benefit oriented and job related:

1. _____

   _____

2. _____

   _____

3. _____

   _____

HOW TO GIVE
FRESH ANSWERS TO STANDARD
INTERVIEW QUESTIONS

Most people welcome standard questions. They are predictable and seemingly easy to answer. The problem is that predictable questions tend to elicit predictable answers—answers that are easy to forget. When an interviewer sees multiple candidates for a position, your interview can become indistinguishable from the rest.

Always be prepared to give specific examples of any benefits stated. It is likely that you will be asked at least a few predictable questions, and you should be prepared to recognize and respond to them with outstanding answers. Take advantage of the predictability, and develop benefits that will impress your interviewer. Again, this is not a question of memorization. It is an exercise in becoming thoroughly familiar with your features and the many different benefits they offer. Don't generalize; be prepared with specifics to back up your claims. Before reading any further, take a few minutes to answer the three questions listed in Exhibit 5-2.

As discussed in Chapter 3, the most common interview question, and the one many interviewers open with, is, "Tell me about yourself." You've already learned how to turn this question around by asking the interviewer for specifics. Now it's time to draw on his or her responses, using all the information you have gleaned from your conversation to help you furnish your answers to standard questions with meaningful benefits. Take a look at the following sample answers and compare them to the responses you wrote in Exhibit 5-2.

Exhibit 5-2 ANSWERING STANDARD QUESTIONS

Learning to answer these simple questions is the key to providing memorable, beneficial answers to any standard question. On the lines below each question, answer with your first, gut response.

What are your strengths?

_____

_____

Why do you want this job?

_____

_____

Why did you leave your last job?

_____

_____

Question: "What are your strengths?"

Answer: "You mentioned that teamwork has been an important part of this company's success [*Shows you have listened well; now you can follow with appropriate features and benefits*]. I have learned that being a good listener [*Feature: Skill, good listener*] is part of what makes me a good team player. I have seen that people at all levels have good ideas [*Feature: Experience*]. I also have learned that a little appreciation goes a long way [*Feature: Skill, offering praise*]. Offering frequent thank-yous can encourage a continual flow of ideas and suggestions [*Benefit: Encourages ongoing flow of ideas*]."

"I know how to express goals and expectations clearly and how to communicate those expectations to my staff [*Feature: Skill, good communicator*]. I have learned that once people know exactly what is expected, they accept the challenges and work hard to meet them [*Benefit: Giving the staff the encouragement and information they need to succeed*]. In addition, I have developed the habit of conducting brief, but regular, team meetings to keep everyone in the loop and working together toward the same goal [*Feature: Skill, developed team-building procedures*]. I found that these meetings kept everyone on track and motivated [*obvious benefit*]."

Question: "Why do you want this job?"

Answer: "When I first heard about this job, I was very interested, and I felt that I would be a perfect fit. I have extensive financial experience, earning my company favorable return on investment and ensuring measurable growth while maintaining proper financial controls [*features*]. I look forward to bringing my thorough knowledge of capital investments, as well as strong sense of ethical responsibility, to a larger, more diversified environment and applying those skills to help improve your bottom line [*benefit*]."

Question: "What are your hobbies?"

Answer: "I have played tennis since I was a kid and compete regularly in local and statewide tournaments [*features*]. Tennis keeps me in shape, both mentally and physically. I usually play early in the morning because it takes only an hour or two, and it helps me work out all my tension. I feel calm and refreshed and carry this with me throughout my workday [*benefit*]."

CHALLENGING QUESTIONS
THAT MEAN THE INTERVIEWER
IS INTERESTED IN YOU

If the interviewer starts to extol the virtues of the company and tries to sell you on why you should take the job, it is pretty obvious that you are at or near the top of the list. This is the best-case scenario. Unfortunately, it's not always clear how the interviewer feels about you.

In the high-stakes game of hiring, it is often difficult to pick the best candidate. In a typical interview situation, it can be almost impossible to determine how a potential employee will react under stress or when left to work unsupervised. I have hired many outside salespeople who would be working in the field with minimal supervision. To test their mettle, I often used a tactic that helped me to learn how a candidate would handle rejection and whether he or she would be persistent in the face of that rejection. Near the end of a successful interview, I would look the candidate in the eye and say, "Well, thanks for coming in, but I don't think you are really what we are looking for."

Most candidates were stunned. After all, up to this point, things had been going along smoothly. Why would I do this at the end of a successful interview to a candidate whom I felt had real potential? Sounds mean, right? It wasn't. You can look at it as a kind of test. The number one issue a salesperson faces on a daily basis is rejection. The successful salesperson stares that rejection down and figures out how to turn it around. He or she figures out how to *find the benefit* that the buyer needs to turn the visit into a sale.

In my example, if a sales candidate shook my hand, thanked me for my time, and headed for the door, I knew that he or she probably would not be successful in sales. In contrast, the candidate who paused and then asked for clarification or for a specific reason why he or she was not right for the job showed that he or she was willing to be persistent. These were benefits that I needed to see before I was willing to hire and train a new salesperson.

I hear those of you who are not in sales moaning again. Trust me, I am not the only hiring manager familiar with these kinds of tactics. They are used in all fields, and when the question comes, it will seem to come out of left field. Watch for that question. It is a good sign. It means the interviewer is really considering you but wants to push a little to see how you respond. There are several questions that fall into this category, and although on the surface they may seem negative, the good news is that they actually indicate a high level of interest on the part of the interviewer.

Knowing what to do in these situations often will clinch you an offer. Again, these questions probably will be asked if the employer is interested in hiring you, so you can be a bit more direct in your answers. Here are a few samples. As you can see, these kinds of questions are *not* restricted to sales.

❏ "Why should we hire you?"

❏ "What part of the job would you have trouble with?"

❏ "I wonder if you really can do this job."

Question: "Why should we hire you?"
Answer: "Hire me because I am the right person for the job. I have worked hard and increased profits in each of the last seven quarters for my company. While I have enjoyed quite a bit of success, I am looking for a more challenging environment. Your company's policy of rewarding employees based on perfor-

mance is exactly the kind of motivation that will encourage me to be even more successful."

Question: "What part of the job would you have trouble with?"

Answer: "I think it will take time to understand your systems, get to know my coworkers, and become familiar with your products and procedures. I know that I must listen first to learn how things work before I can make changes or suggestions. By listening, I will be learning how things are done here and helping my staff become comfortable with my style and presence. By encouraging them to come forth with their ideas, I will become a productive manager."

Question: "I wonder if you really can do this job."

Believe it or not, when you hear this, you can be pretty sure the interviewer is interested in hiring you. If he or she really felt that you were *not* right for the job, he or she would thank you for your time and show you the door. The interviewer would not be wasting his or her time by inviting you to continue the conversation. An interviewer chooses to use this kind of statement when he or she wants you to *help* him or her hire you; so use your skills to find out what he or she is really asking, and be prepared to wow the interviewer with your best features and benefits.

By this point in the meeting, you have spent quite a bit of time with the interviewer and have developed a meaningful rapport. You might respond with a simple prompt, "Oh?" or a leading statement such as, "I am surprised to hear you say that. The more we talked, the more I felt that I had the skills, experience, and drive necessary to succeed in this position, and I thought you shared that assessment."

The interviewer probably would respond with a clarifying statement such as, "I'm concerned about whether you could succeed with us because all your experience has been in public and academic libraries, and this is a private, for-profit company looking for a research librarian."

Then you could say with a smile

"Ms. Jones, my years of library experience have given me the opportunity to research a broad range of subjects for people at all levels of interest and proficiency, from the youngest readers to professors conducting cutting-edge scientific investigations. I hear your concern about this being a different environment [*Your active listening skills reflect back her concerns*], but I know that after a short learning period, I will become familiar with your company, its products, and its research needs. The important thing is that I understand the research process and have kept current with the latest in research technologies. I recognize that each staff member here will tap the librarian for different kinds of information [*feature*] and that my listening skills will help me find the information that is important to each one [*benefit*].

"In addition, I have a successful history of planning and implementing library programs. As you can see, last year I was named the Academic/Research Librarian of the Year by the Association of College and Resource Librarians [*Show commendation. Note that these two sentences present features*]. I feel strongly that I could help your company develop its research collection and encourage your staff to use it to its maximum potential [*benefit*]. So, even though the environment is different, my understanding of research techniques will ensure successful results [*benefit*]."

Stop, smile, and pause for a response. If the interviewer is silent, you might add, "Have I addressed your concerns, or should I continue with more specifics?"

SALARY CONVERSATIONS THAT GIVE YOU INFORMATION

Many interview guides tell you not to discuss salary during the first interview, but you may not have a choice. Job applications frequently ask your current salary and preferred salary range. Gatekeepers—such as human resources representatives and headhunters—often will ask for your current salary as a condition of continuing on in the interview process.

What should you do if the interviewer asks your salary? If you simply answer with the dollar amount, you are nowhere. You don't know

❏ The salary range for the position

❏ Whether you are within that range, above it, or below it

❏ What role benefits play in the total compensation package

You may say: "My salary is $60,000 plus benefits. I assume that this is within the salary range for this job?"

If the answer is: "Our range for this job is $45,000 to $55,000," you might respond with

"I assume that there is some flexibility."

or

> "If we feel that we can be good for each other, I can
> be a bit flexible. Can you also be flexible?"

Stop talking and listen for tone and attitude. If the answer is "No," but you are still interested in the job, you might ask if it is possible to negotiate a salary review after the first three months, concluding with, "I feel confident that I will do a good job that will make you very happy."

It is important to recognize where you stand in this situation and remain in control. Don't forget to take company benefits into consideration—both those you receive from your present employer and those offered by the prospective company. Some employers include valuable benefits that could make the total compensation package much more attractive, including such things as health and life insurance, tuition reimbursement, health club membership, vacation, profit sharing, and retirement plans.

Remember that it is an exercise in futility to try to memorize answers to interview questions. There are simply too many questions and too many variations to each question to make this worthwhile. By practicing the skills you have learned in Chapters 1 through 5, you will be prepared to answer any question you may be asked. By responding with confidence in your own words, you will feel comfortable and in control. That confidence will show in your answers, and you will be rewarded with an offer for a job you want.

RATE YOURSELF

To see if you are ready to move on, rate yourself on each of the questions in Exhibit 5-3 using a scale of 1 to 10. If you score 7 or better on every question, continue on to Chapter 6.

Exhibit 5-3 RATE YOURSELF: HOW WELL DO YOU
ANSWER TOUGH QUESTIONS?

	Rating (1–10)
Do I understand why I should not try to memorize answers to interview questions?	_____
Do I know what my most hated question is?	_____
Have I learned to welcome my most hated question as an opportunity?	_____
Do I know how to make the most of my answers to standard interview questions?	_____
Can I recognize questions that indicate that the interviewer is interested in me?	_____
Do my answers do more than simply reiterate my résumé?	_____
Do I know how to respond to salary-related questions?	_____

....

CHAPTER 6

Getting and Maximizing References and Referrals

It's not what you know,
but who you know.

—Old saying

NETWORKING YOUR WAY TO THE TOP

Contacts, referrals, and references are the lifeblood of any job search. It's up to you to build and maintain an effective network of contacts. The more people who know about your job search, the better.

Who are your *contacts*? The simple answer is that anyone can be a contact. Obviously, mentors, supervisors, and teachers are important contacts, but don't limit yourself to the obvious. Your sister's roommate, your dentist's brother-in-law, or your father's golf buddy are all potential contacts. The key is to tell people you are looking for a job. Sometimes this requires discretion, but the more people who know what you do and what you want in a job, the better. Your goal is to get a referral. A *referral* is when one of your contacts, no matter how tenuous the relationship, lets you know of a job opening or of another potential contact in your field.

Joining a professional or trade association is an excellent way to expand your list of professional contacts. Many of these organizations offer social functions during meetings and conventions for the purpose of networking. Your listening skills will be valuable here. Everyone at a networking event is looking for something, so you should spend more time listening than talking. Learn to summarize your career objectives into a 30- to 40-second sound bite that ends with a benefit, and wait for questions before you provide more details. Be sure to carry business cards and hand them out at these events.

Simple thank-you notes go a long way toward making a lasting positive impression on your contacts. Send a note to a former mentor thanking her for something she taught you. Let her know how your career has progressed, and ask her to get in touch with you if she hears of any openings that may be of interest. Anytime you make a change in your contact information (such as moving, getting a new home or cell phone number, or changing jobs), it is a good time to touch base with the important people in your network.

If someone refers you to a company or an opening, call or e-mail him and ask for as much information as possible about the position, the people, and the company. Ask whether he knows anyone in the company and, if so, how you can reach them and if you can use your contact's name. A referral puts you 10 steps ahead in the game. You are no longer just some unknown applying to a blind newspaper ad or job board—

you have an inside track. Be professional in following up on any referrals; you want to make your contact look good. To maintain a strong working relationship with an obliging contact, be sure to send thank-you notes for anything he does to help you along the way.

Once you have moved on to a new position, drop an occasional e-mail to the important people you know within your field to keep them apprised of your career changes. As always, be sure to thank them for any help they have provided, and offer to be of help to them in any way you can. And remember that networking goes both ways. Keep your ears open for opportunities that may benefit one of your contacts. You will be remembered in kind.

REFERENCES—ASK FIRST

At the end of most résumés, you see the phrase "References available on request." What is the benefit of that? Don't wait for a request. Have your references lined up and ready to go before you send out your first résumé.

A *reference* is someone who is willing to supply a spoken or written recommendation of you and your work. You must always *ask* people if they are willing to serve as reference. Do not assume that someone will provide you with a good reference unless you have consulted with him or her first. Think about the people in your past who might serve as positive references. Contact them, and let them know about your job search. Ask if they are willing to serve as a reference and how they would prefer to be contacted (e.g., telephone, e-mail, etc.). Next, ask if they would be willing to write a letter of reference for you to have on file. This can be an impressive introduction to your skills and benefits during an interview.

If you are newly out of school, look to professors, internship sponsors, managers from part-time jobs, and even supervisors of volunteer programs where you have made a mark. For more seasoned workers, the bulk of your references should be professional. Your Aunt Mary may think that you are the greatest thing since sliced bread, but if she has never employed you, then her recommendation won't mean much to a prospective employer. When you are looking for a job while still working, it is often difficult or impossible to ask your current boss for a reference. Now is the time to reconnect with past supervisors who know you and appreciate your work.

MAKE IT EASY FOR YOUR REFERENCES

When you ask someone to write a letter of reference or recommendation, they may willingly agree, but in our busy world, the best intentions can get sidetracked. Writing a reference is probably not on top of anyone's "to do" list, and a week or two may go by without a response, causing critical delays in your job search.

I propose a different method. Once your reference has agreed to write a letter of reference or recommendation, say: "Thanks, I know this is a nuisance, but I think I can make it a little easier. I don't want to be presumptuous, but may I e-mail some of the points you might make? Obviously, you are welcome to make corrections, deletions, or additions as you see fit. After I hear back from you, I can put the material with your revisions in letter format and send it back for your signature."

As you compose your list of points, be sure to phrase them in terms of features and benefits. Take everything you have learned in this book and make your list stand out, ending each phrase with a benefit. Limit your list of points to the features and benefits that your reference knows and will feel comfortable confirming. Remind your reference of the specifics of your working relationship so that he or she doesn't have to dig into his or her files or memories for the facts.

It's important that any reference letters be printed on business stationery. Most letterhead requires a two-inch margin at the top and one-and-a-quarter-inch margins on the bottom and sides. Setting up your reference material in letter format with appropriate margins makes it easy for your reference to print it, sign it, and mail it. Note in your e-mail that you have sent by "snail mail" a self-addressed envelope (at least 9 by 12 inches) with adequate postage to return the signed letter to you. You may want to ask for three or four signed original copies.

How many letters do you need? The obvious answer is as many as you can get. Although 10 letters would be overkill (and probably impossible), it will look more impressive if you have four or five or even eight excellent letters from different sources than if you have only one or two. Put the most impressive letter on top. Be sure to make copies of every reference letter, and never give away your last copy!

Use the worksheet in Exhibit 6-1 when developing the points for your references to use in a letter of recommendation. Most companies want to contact references directly. You should ask your references if they would mind forwarding a copy of their letters or e-mails to you for your files.

Exhibit 6-1 GUIDELINES FOR REFERENCES

Use this blank worksheet to provide your references with vital information about your features and benefits. Choose three or four features and provide specific benefits that you want your reference to use when talking or writing about you. Your reference will not have any idea what is important to the interviewer, so you need to identify an appropriate benefit for each feature you would like your reference to address.

Your information	Your name:	
	Address:	
	Phone number:	
	E-mail:	
	Current employer:	
	Current position:	
	Relationship to reference: (include dates, if applicable)	
Information about the job/ company	Contact name and position:	
	Company name:	
	Address:	
	Phone number:	
	E-mail:	
	Job title or description:	
Features and benefits	**Feature**	**Appropriate Benefit**
Include	☐ Your résumé ☐ Business card	

HOW TO MAXIMIZE LETTERS OF RECOMMENDATION AND REFERRALS

Once you have collected letters from your supporters, what do you do with them? My suggestion is to invest in a leather binder or portfolio and put your referrals in plastic sleeves. Take this portfolio with you to every interview. Ask your interviewer if you could present some letters that explain how people feel about you. Then open the binder and show the references. Although it is difficult to judge how long an interview will last, it is usually more effective to present your references at the beginning or in the middle of the conversation. If you wait until the end you will have missed an opportunity for further discussion.

As the interview is drawing to a close, remind the interviewer about the specific benefits of having you on his or her team. Before you leave, give the interviewer a list of your references, on a separate piece of paper, with names, titles, company names and addresses, phone numbers, and e-mail addresses. Be sure that your name and contact information is listed at the top—in case your reference list gets separated from your résumé.

As you offer this list to your interviewer, encourage the interviewer to contact your references. This is one of the few areas where you have some control during the interview process. You have already contacted your references and know that they will provide positive feedback that will reinforce the benefits of hiring you. Encouraging the interviewer to contact these great resources will give you another chance to stand out from the crowd.

The interviewer's reaction also could be a clue about interest you have generated. If he or she accepts your reference list eagerly or asks for more information about your references, it is a good sign that you have made a favorable impression.

After the interview (but on the same day), contact your references to tell them that they may be contacted by a potential employer. Refer to the completed "Guidelines for References" worksheet in Exhibit 6-1, being sure to include the name of the company, the position for which you're being considered, and the names of your contacts (i.e., the interviewer and anyone else you met) so that your references will recognize and be prepared for the call when it comes. Offer one or two benefits that you would like your reference to emphasize. Keep all your references informed as to how your search is going. Tell them where you are interviewing, and ask if they have any contacts or leads that may be helpful.

Sending thank-you letters after the interview is a vital part of the process. One important attachment should be your list of references. Even if you handed your references to the interviewer, attach another copy to your thank-you note. Remember that the interviewer could be seeing many candidates and may not always remember the specifics of your interview. (For more information on thank-you notes, see Chapter 8.)

Be sure to send a thank-you note to your references as well, especially if they have provided you with a letter of recommendation. Send them a copy of your résumé, and ask them to keep you in mind if they hear of any opportunities in your field.

RATE YOURSELF

Before you move ahead, take a moment to rate yourself in each of the areas from this chapter. Use Exhibit 6-2, and rate yourself on a scale of 1 to 10. Once you have scored at least 7 in each of these areas, then you can move on to Chapter 7.

Exhibit 6-2 RATE YOURSELF: HOW WELL ARE YOU
USING YOUR REFERENCES?

	Rating (1–10)
• Do I understand that I must ask people to serve as references before I give out their contact information?	_____
• Do I know how to make it easier for someone to provide me with a letter of recommendation?	_____
• Do I understand how to use good references to their maximum potential during and after an interview?	_____
• Do I value establishing and maintaining long-term professional networks?	_____
• Did I contact my references to tell them of my interview, inform them of a possible call, and ask them to emphasize the important benefits?	_____

CHAPTER 7

How to Prepare for Different Interview Situations

It ain't over til it's over.

—Yogi Berra

Make no mistake—the hiring company will spend both time and money preparing to interview you. Your résumé will be reviewed by people within the company, as well as possibly by outside consultants. Many companies conduct background checks, and almost all will check out your Internet presence. See Chapter 8 for information on how to protect your image, including on the Web. Let's take a look now at some of the people who will investigate you for the hiring company before you even set foot in the door.

WHO WILL INTERVIEW YOU FIRST?

As noted earlier, there are many types of interviewers. Some have little experience, and others are well trained. You probably will interview with several people within a company before you are offered a job. Each one has different experiences, expectations, motives, and needs. You cannot choose your interviewer, so it is best to be prepared for all circumstances. Here are just a few of the kinds of people you might interview with along the way.

Interviewing with an Executive Recruiter or Headhunter

This is not the cannibal from old movies; instead, a *headhunter* in the world of job hunting is someone who has been contracted as a consultant by the hiring company to find the right person for a specific job. The terms *recruiter* and *headhunter* are interchangeable. In general, although a headhunter may not know all the specifics of a particular job or industry, he or she is very experienced at vetting (i.e., determining the suitability of candidates). Some headhunters have long-standing relationships with the hiring company; others are hired on an as-needed basis. Many headhunters specialize in specific industries or skill areas.

Generally speaking, headhunters contact you, not the other way around. Recruiters cast big nets to develop a list of potential candidates for their files. They often will keep your name on file for years, especially if you are in an industry in which they specialize. Communicate your skills in terms of benefits, and a recruiter will keep your name on the top of his or her list.

If you are contacted by a headhunter, use *closed* probes to gather information. (Go back to Chapter 4 to refresh yourself on the difference between open- and closed-probe questions.) First, ask whether the headhunter is contacting you about a specific job and, if so, how long the position has been open and how the opening occurred. Then, using your soft questioning skills, ask the headhunter to tell you a little about the company (its makeup, size, products, culture, etc.). It's a good idea to prepare a brief list of questions for headhunters and keep it handy. Your questions convey important information to the headhunter about your interviewing skills. They also allow you to find out what is important to both the head-hunter and the hiring company, which will enable you to craft your answers with appropriate benefits.

Remember, an outside recruiter usually is paid by the hiring company when a placement is made, and his or her commission often is based on the salary of the new hire. In other words, the more money *you* make, the more money the head-hunter makes. Therefore, the headhunter probably will ask you to disclose your current salary or at least give a range. Remember, salary is just one part of your compensation package, so be sure to include any benefits that are particularly important to you. Also discuss whether you are willing to relocate and if you have any restrictions in terms of geographic location.

Interviewing with an In-House Recruiter

This person is likely to be on staff at a large company. When approached by an in-house recruiter, you should again listen carefully, and ask the same kinds of closed-probe questions you would pose to a headhunter. If the company is looking to fill a particular opening and you don't quite fit the bill, the recruiter may ask to keep your name on file. You want to build bridges here, so be polite and courteous.

The primary difference between contract recruiters and in-house recruiters is that an in-house recruiter is much more interested in weeding you out than in adding you to a list of potential candidates. Again, communicating your benefits is the best way to position yourself with an in-house recruiter.

Interviewing with Human Resources (HR) Personnel

An HR manager is usually the first person in a company to see your résumé. His or her primary job is to *weed you out*. If you get a call or an e-mail from an HR manager, keep in mind that what you say and how you say it will determine whether you move forward in the process or are eliminated on the spot.

Although the HR manager is usually not the final decision maker, he or she does wield a great deal of power—particularly at the beginning of the process—because he or she will decide whether or not you get an interview. Therefore, you must make a good impression. Let the manager know that you are interested in the company and the position by using specifics from your research. Again, use your excellent listening skills and soft questions to hone in on which benefits are important to him or her and the department he or she is representing.

Establish a Good Relationship to Get to the *Next* Interview

These three professionals—headhunters, recruiters, and HR managers—serve as screeners for the hiring manager. They want to send only the best, most desirable, and qualified candidates on to be interviewed by the hiring manager and his or her team. By establishing a good relationship with these individuals, you can move yourself along to the next step in the process.

In addition, headhunters, recruiters, and HR people are valuable sources of information. Here are some questions they may be able to answer for you:

❑ "Who will be at the interview?"

❑ "What are the interviewers' names and positions?"

❑ "Who is the senior person in the group?"

❑ "What is the management hierarchy—who reports to whom?"

❑ "Who is the decision maker?"

❑ With a smile, ask the recruiter, "How can I make you look good?"

❑ "Is there anything else I should know before the interview?"

❑ End with the open probe, "What's the process?"

WHAT YOU NEED TO KNOW ABOUT THE "REAL" INTERVIEW

This is what you have been waiting for! You have finally reached what is commonly thought of as the "job interview." Everything you have done up to this point—the research, the résumé writing, the cover letter, the screening interviews—all comes down to this interview, the most detailed and challenging part of the process.

Interviewing with the Hiring Manager

The hiring manager likely will be your future boss and is the ultimate decision maker. By the time you reach this point in the hiring process, your résumé will already have passed an initial screening, and you may have had one or more interviews (by phone or in person) with HR or recruiting personnel. Unlike the other professionals you have encountered along the way who conduct interviews daily, the hiring manager may or may not be a skilled interviewer. He or she does, however, have in-depth knowledge of the company, the department, and the position. More important, he or she will decide whether or not you get this job.

Here are some things you need to know about the hiring manager so that you can use all the skills you have learned to their greatest advantage during this interview. If this interviewer will be your boss, he or she will want to know the answers to the following questions in addition to your skills and experiences:

1. Can you make your boss look good?

2. What new strengths do you bring to the team?

3. How will you fit in with the existing team?

4. How will you get along with one another?

5. How well will you take direction?

6. Are you a possible threat to his or her job?

7. Are you reliable?

In addition to being responsible for filling the job opening, the hiring manager also usually develops the job description by

❑ Establishing major responsibilities

❑ Delineating what talent, experience, and skills are required

❑ Determining the preferred background of potential candidates

The interviewer probably will be familiar with your résumé and basic background by the time you meet and now will be focusing on the following questions and behaviors:

❏ How relaxed (or nervous) are you?

❏ How do you handle questions?

❏ Are you prepared?

❏ How much knowledge do you have of the company, the industry, and the job requirements?

❏ How well do you communicate verbally?

❏ How well do you communicate nonverbally (i.e., warmth, smiles, voice, confidence, eye contact, and posture)?

❏ How good are your listening skills?

❏ Do you ask good questions?

❏ Is your personality a good fit for the company and for the department?

❏ What is the general feeling about you during the interview? Does that feeling change after the interview?

Sometimes a company will devote an entire day to interviewing you, scheduling meetings with several members of the department and other higher-ups in the management chain. Every interviewer has a wish list of skills, experiences, and personality traits that he or she would like an applicant to possess. The list changes depending on the interviewer and his or her position, and it is unlikely that any one candidate will fulfill every wish. Your job during the interview is to try to determine the *most important* areas by

❏ Asking soft questions (refer to Chapter 4 for some examples of these)

❏ Listening carefully to the answers

❏ Learning what benefits are valuable to each interviewer

Keep track of what you learn during each phase of the interview, and carry that information with you to the next phase. Remember, though, that you still must address the needs of *each individual interviewer.*

Be on your toes even during "down times" throughout the interview day. Everything the hiring manager does is related to finding the person who can do the best job. Small talk, gaps in conversation, hard-ball questions, and seemingly off-handed remarks are all tools to get you to reveal more about who you are and what you have to offer. Remember, the interviewer is looking for the candidate who offers the most benefits; again, it's all about "What will you do for *me*?"

Moving Up the Chain of Command

As you move through a number of interviews in the day, keep in mind that different interviewers will be looking for different benefits. If you interview with a top-management person—for example, your boss's boss—he or she may be looking for such qualities as

1. Can you make your boss look good?

2. Are you promotable?

3. Will you relocate if necessary?

4. Could you possibly do your present boss's job in the future?

5. Are you a wise investment for the company?

Meeting with Coworkers

On the other hand, a coworker will have yet another set of criteria:

1. Can you make your coworker look good?

2. Are you a threat?

3. Will you pull your weight?

4. Will you get along together?

It is no coincidence that the first question on the mind of each member of the interview team is whether or not you can make him or her look good. Again, this is another way of asking: "What will you do for *me*?" Answer this question for each interviewer with the right benefits, and you *will* get the job offer.

Beyond Your Résumé—Emphasizing Benefits from Other Work or Life Experiences

Here is an example of how you can reach beyond your résumé to address some of the universal qualities that most employers value. Let's say that you are interviewing for a job as a computer programmer. In the past, you spent some time digging ditches. Would you mention this in the interview? Most people would say no; this has nothing to do with getting a computer programming job.

I say that this is a mistake. You can use this seemingly unrelated experience to highlight some valuable benefits. Focus on what you have discovered about your interviewer's priorities during the conversation thus far, and make your points relevant. For example, let's say that the interviewer has indicated that a strong work ethic is something he values highly. You could say: "I was a ditch digger when I was going to school to help pay my expenses, so you know that I am no stranger to hard work. I assure you that I will bring this same intensity to work for you."

If the interviewer has emphasized the importance of teamwork, you might say: "I worked digging ditches with a lot of different kinds of people. I learned that our safety and ability to accomplish the job depended on how well we worked together as a team. That's the attitude I bring to all my work—that teamwork is a key ingredient to success."

Let's say that the interviewer has told you that some projects require long hours and occasional weekends: "Digging ditches required us to work different shifts—early mornings, late into the night, and on weekends—in all kinds of weather. I know the value of being flexible, and I am dedicated to getting the job done."

In each example, you have used your experience from an unrelated job to present a benefit that is valuable to the job at hand. Take some time now to review your own background, looking for similar benefits in your past that you never thought of mentioning during an interview. Take a fresh look at

❏ Volunteer activities

❏ Internships and part-time jobs outside your field

❏ Sports and hobbies

❏ Relevant household management skills (budgeting, time management, etc.)

HOW TO HANDLE GROUP INTERVIEWS

Instead of or in addition to consecutive interviews, it is possible that you may be interviewed by several people at one time, each looking for different and specific benefits in a candidate. This can be tricky. You have to address the needs of *every person in the room* without contradicting yourself or seeming like you are trying to be all things to all people. A financial manager's interest in a candidate, for example, will be different from a marketing specialist's—so how can you provide meaningful benefits to each of them?

If you know in advance that you will be participating in a group interview, ask your contact for some basic information. Recruiters and headhunters can be particularly helpful in this situation. It is in their best interest for you to do well during an interview, so feel free to ask direct questions about the company and the interviewers. Any inside information you can gather from these professionals will help you to communicate appropriate benefits during the interview.

A group interview is demanding and will require that you use all your skills to help determine what benefits are most important to the individuals in the room, as well as to the group as a whole. Take a few notes as you go to help you remember names and important issues. Although you want to address each individual's needs with an appropriate benefit, you must take care not to concentrate too much on any one individual at the expense of others. At the end of the interview, be sure to make eye contact with each person individually and thank them separately. Afterward, send individual thank-you notes to each person in the group. (For more details on writing thank-you notes, see Chapter 8.)

WHAT YOU NEED TO KNOW ABOUT SECOND INTERVIEWS

A second interview is different from an initial interview. In general, if you are invited back for a second interview, you can be sure the company is interested in you. It usually means that you have passed through to the next, often last step in the hiring process. A second interview may mean that the company has reduced the number of candidates to a small group of finalists, and it needs additional information to make a decision. Other times, a second interview means that your candidacy is being given a final stamp of approval and that negotiations are ready to begin.

In either situation, you probably will meet with the hiring manager again, and this may be when you meet his or her supervisor for the first time. In this case, the interviewer who invited you back will have a vested interest in your performance during the second interview. In a sense, your success or failure will be a reflection of the hiring manager's interviewing skills. If you have a few private minutes, gently ask the first interviewer if he or she has any hints or advice for you when you meet his or her supervisor.

Preparing for the second interview starts immediately after the first interview is over. Chapter 8 discusses in detail how to conduct your own performance review after each interview and includes the "Interview Review Form," which has been designed to help you with this postinterview self-evaluation. It's vital to know where you stumble, as well as what you did well enough to warrant being invited back for a second interview. The review will help you to remember what you said and enable you to address your weak spots, as well as reemphasize the benefits that impressed your interviewer the first time around.

If you worked with a recruiter or headhunter, contact that person too, and go over any trouble spots from the first interview. Ask whether the recruiter has received any feedback that will help you to prepare for a second interview or if the recruiter would be willing to rehearse with you. The recruiter or headhunter also may have information about who will be present during the second interview and what the parameters are for negotiating salary and benefits.

When I conducted second interviews, I always started with, "You must have lots of questions." So be prepared. Do more research on the company, and develop a new set of questions. In a second interview, you can be more specific and direct with your questions by asking about the particulars of the job:

❑ "What is the chain of command?"

❑ "When would you need me to start?"

❑ "How and when do you conduct performance evaluations?"

❑ "What is the compensation package?"

Soft questions and leading statements (described in detail in Chapter 4) will continue to play an important role in the second interview, allowing you to gather more information about the specific wants and needs of the interviewer. When answering questions, you should have a clearer idea of what is important and be able to end each statement with a specific benefit.

It is important to send thank-you notes again after a second interview. Go back and complete another "Interview Review Form" (Exhibit 8-1) before writing out your thank-you notes. This will help you to focus on the benefits you present in the note, allowing you to emphasize a point you made during the interview or offer something you may have forgotten or did not have an opportunity to discuss.

DEALING WITH MEAL INTERVIEWS

As if interviewing weren't stressful enough, sometimes you are expected to interview and eat at the same time. Don't be fooled into thinking that interviewing over a meal is somehow more casual or less serious than other forms of interviewing. A meal interview may be scheduled for convenience, or it may be set up to see how you function as a professional in social situations. In any case, you need to use all your skills—as well as your best manners—during an interview that involves food.

The distractions of the meal, especially in a restaurant, mean that you must pay even closer attention to your interviewer to determine what is important to him or her. Here are a few tips for navigating the treacherous waters of a breakfast, lunch, or dinner interview:

❏ Order a medium-priced meal that is simple to eat (no finger foods, no messy sauces).

❏ Avoid alcohol.

❏ Use your best listening skills, and maintain eye contact as much as possible.

❏ Don't forget to answer questions using features and benefits.

❏ Convey that you like the restaurant (or food that has been brought in). Remember, the interviewer made this choice.

❏ Remember that even casual conversations are being used to evaluate you as a potential employee.

❏ If you have only a shaky grasp of the niceties of eating in a fancy restaurant, brush up before you go, and when in doubt, follow the lead of your host.

PREPARING FOR "ELEVATOR INTERVIEWS"

The ability to convey your experience and career goals briefly and succinctly is an important skill. Even if you aren't looking to make a move (yet), this skill will help you to keep your career goals in mind and allow you to express them whenever you make a new contact. Spend time thinking about this information, and practice this skill until you are able to communicate your benefits in a few brief sentences.

This is sometimes called an "elevator interview" because you should be able to complete the entire statement in the time it takes for an average elevator ride. It is a vital tool to have at your disposal when talking to recruiters and headhunters, especially at job fairs. Mastering the elevator interview is a valuable networking tool.

Use the worksheet in Exhibit 7-1 to develop your talking points for an elevator interview. Remember, your time is brief, one minute at the most. Hit your most important

Exhibit 7-1 ELEVATOR INTERVIEW WORKSHEET

Your information	Your name:	
	Current position:	
	Career goal:	
	Feature	**Appropriate Benefit**
Features and benefits		
Include	☐ Business card	

features and their most valuable benefits. You must practice your elevator interview over and over until you can do it smoothly and with confidence.

SURVIVING JOB FAIRS

Job fairs present a unique interviewing situation. Most often job fairs are hosted by colleges and universities, professional associations and industry groups, or governmental bodies (such as municipalities, states or counties, or administrative agencies). They usually take place in large venues, such as halls or hotels. Different companies and hiring agencies send HR staff to act as recruiters.

A job fair may last several hours or several days. It can be an exhausting and frustrating experience—unless you are prepared. Here are some tools that will help you to navigate the fair, narrow your focus, and stand out in the crowd:

1. Arrive early, at the beginning of the day, if possible. Interviewers will be fresh, the fair will be less crowded, and first impressions can be lasting ones.

2. When you first arrive, review the companies and jobs available. Decide which booths to visit, and rank them in order of importance to you. Then look at the map, determine where your top prospects are located, and plan to go there first. Set up a rough schedule to maximize the efficiency of your day. If you register early, ask for any materials that may be available ahead of time.

3. The interviewers at job fairs are usually HR personnel, especially if they represent a large firm. A smaller company, however, may not have an HR department, and the

interviewer actually might do the hiring. Always be prepared, and give each interviewer your best effort.

4. If a company appeals to you, but the job openings listed do not, you still should plan to visit the booth. When you approach the interviewer, smile, be polite, explain your situation, and give him or her your résumé. Ask for a card and the name of the person you should contact in the future.

5. When standing in line waiting your turn, listen intently to what is going on in front of you. You could learn a lot, especially about the role of the interviewer. You also may be able to hear questions asked of people ahead of you and prepare your answers to include an appropriate benefit from your own experience.

6. Take copies of your résumé and other materials, including a pen and paper in a nice case. Carrying loose papers gets cumbersome and sloppy, and it creates a poor image.

7. Treat this interview with the same intensity you would if it were in an office. Job fair interviews usually serve as a screening process. If you impress the interviewer, it may give you an opportunity to go to the next level.

8. Smiles are always important, but they are essential at a job fair. The interviewer has seen so many people over the course of the day that a smile really goes miles to make you memorable.

9. Ask who and when you should call to follow up on the interview, and ask for a business card.

10. When the interview is over, repeat the benefits you bring. Ask: "What is the process?" Then offer the interviewer

a list of references with phone numbers and e-mail addresses. It is also a good idea to print out some business cards with your contact information. You can purchase sheets of blank business cards at any office supply store, and templates are available for most word-processing programs.

11. Try to be around near the end of the job fair and return to the companies that interest you most. During any spare time at the fair, write a thank-you note, and give it to your interviewer *on the spot*. He or she will be impressed and may give you a chance to talk some more.

12. Dress is important in this situation because many job seekers at these fairs are very casual. *Proper* dress will help you to stand out in the crowd.

13. Job fairs are usually long and exhausting. Eat a good breakfast before you go. Wear comfortable shoes because you likely will be on your feet most of the time, and choose clothes that will stay crisp all day. Finally, take occasional breaks to eat, freshen up, or recompose yourself.

UNDERSTAND THE INTERVIEWING AND HIRING PROCESS

Conducting a search to fill an open position is an expensive, time-consuming process for a hiring company. The company wants to make sure that it hires the right person the first time. Headhunters, recruiters, and HR staff often are used to streamline the process, and they can eliminate you from the running before you even get to the interview stage. You can be sure that these professionals will be doing their homework about you, so make sure that you do the same. Be prepared for the call. Keep an organized list of ads you have answered and résumés you have sent, along with any information you have gathered about the company.

Recognize that filling a position is a *process*. It takes time. You may be asked to participate in several different types of interviews along the way—anything from a quick phone call to set up an interview appointment, to a lengthy phone interview, to one or more face-to-face interviews. Each step in the process is designed to weed out candidates. You must be prepared and professional every step of the way to earn the job offer.

Remember that different interviewers have different needs and objectives. It is your job to determine those needs and answer them with appropriate benefits. Different types of interviews—from group meetings to job fairs and interviews over a meal to second interviews—present different challenges and opportunities.

RATE YOURSELF

Before you move ahead to the next chapter, be sure you understand the concepts presented here. Keep in mind that this chapter builds on everything you have learned so far, so you may need to review earlier chapters before you can feel comfortable with everything presented here. Rate yourself using the worksheet in Exhibit 7-2 in each area on a scale of 1 to 10. Once you have scored at least 7 in each of these areas, then you can move on to the final chapter.

Exhibit 7-2 RATE YOURSELF: HOW PREPARED ARE YOU TO BE INTERVIEWED BY DIFFERENT TYPES OF INTERVIEWERS AND IN DIFFERENT SITUATIONS?

Rating (1–10)

- Do I understand the primary responsibility of headhunters, recruiters, and HR staff in the interview process? _____

- Do I understand that different interviewers have different skill levels and different agendas? _____

- Do I understand how to determine the needs of each interviewer and how to address those needs with different benefits? _____

- Have I examined all my life experiences for benefits that may be valuable for an employer? _____

- Do I understand the challenges of interviewing in different situations (e.g., job fairs, second interviews, meal interviews, and group interviews)? _____

CHAPTER 8

The Interview—Before, During, and After

There are no secrets to success.
It is the result of preparation, hard work,
and learning from failure.

—Colin Powell

This book is devoted to the specifics of using features and benefits during the interview process to improve your chances of getting the job you want. There are numerous resources available that will help you to produce a winning résumé, dress for success, and follow up with thank-you notes. This chapter touches on these issues briefly, only as they relate to the use of features and benefits.

BEFORE THE INTERVIEW

Every job search starts with a résumé. Yours needs to be great. Use active verbs and actual statistics. The more you can quantify your accomplishments, the better qualified you'll seem for the job you want. Develop a clear, concise résumé, and have it reviewed by as many people as possible before you send it out. Make sure that it is clean and legible and has absolutely no mistakes. It is a general truth that résumés with mistakes (even small typographical errors) end up in the wastebasket. Employers don't have time to waste on someone who did not even bother to make a perfect first impression. These suggestions may seem like basic good advice, but you wouldn't believe how many smart, well-educated people prepare sloppy, dreadful résumés—and think that they're just fine!

It is usually helpful to have more than one version of your résumé. In fact, if you are searching in more than one arena (e.g., for-profit companies and nonprofit organizations) or more than one industry, it is essential to have a targeted résumé for each category. Your skills and experiences will be the same; you will just present them differently, highlighting the most pertinent information and slanting your benefits to meet the needs of the targeted organizations.

The purpose of a résumé is to get you past the gatekeepers and closer to an interview. Once you have a first interview scheduled, your résumé has done its job—the rest is up to you. Having said that, I would suggest that your résumé presents your features (i.e., your skills and experiences) in a short format, often bulleted and in chronological order—but it's critical that you know each one of those features and facts by heart, and even more important, you need to be able to attach an appropriate benefit to each one.

Use everything you know about the job and the company when composing your cover letter. Once you have chosen which version of your résumé to use, write your cover letter highlighting a few appropriate features and benefits. Your cover letter is often the first opportunity you have to set yourself apart from the other applicants by emphasizing your benefits.

\

Researching the Company
That's Interviewing You Is Critical

Knowing that you don't know is knowing. When y(
nize that you don't know everything, you can

❏ Do your homework before the interview.

❏ Work on becoming a good listener during the interview.

❏ Ask good questions.

Chapter 3 discussed the importance of doing research on the company and interviewer(s) before you meet. But why do you need to do research? Aren't they supposed to be learning about you? If you still believe this, go directly to the beginning of this book and begin again—do not pass GO; do not collect $200.

Researching the company provides you with specific information that you can use during an interview to talk about how you will be a benefit to the organization. For example, if you know the company's rank within the industry, you can tell how your experience will allow you to maintain or improve that rank. You will impress the interviewer with your industry knowledge, as well as with how you, personally, will be an asset to the company. If you know about a particular success that the interviewer has achieved, the interviewer will be flattered by your knowledge of him or her, and you will be able to show how your experience will be a benefit to the specific business interests that are important to *him* or *her*. Research allows you to be confident and specific. For example:

> "I read that you recently received the Wilks Memorial Award from the American Statistical Association. That is quite an honor. I joined the student

branch of the ASA as an undergraduate and attended several excellent seminars at last year's Joint Statistical Meetings. In addition to reading the *Journal* regularly, I find that these seminars keep me up to date on the latest research in the field."

In this example, your research uncovered that the interviewer has received a prestigious award. This background information has allowed you to display your knowledge of the award and what it represents, compliment the interviewer on her achievement, show your involvement in the awarding organization (which is obviously important to the interviewer), and end with a benefit of what *you* can offer to the company interviewing you. This is a pretty powerful combination of features and benefits to be able to deliver in just a few sentences.

Your research will continue as you walk into the building and even into the interviewer's office. Be aware of your surroundings. Notice personal objects and photographs that can give you a clue about what is important to the interviewer. If the business sponsors a Little League baseball team, there frequently will be plaques in the lobby. If the interviewer's office is decorated with theater playbills, you may have discovered his interest in the performing arts.

But don't assume anything: Maybe the decorative objects were left over from the last tenant of the office. Use your questioning skills to probe further and get more information about what is truly important to the interviewer before you go off on a tangent. For example, you could use a leading statement such as, "You certainly have an interesting collection of playbills." If your interviewer explains that all the pictures in the office were supplied by the decorator, you know that the playbills are not important to him. On the other hand, he might say something like, "Thank you. I am a huge theater buff and have been collecting playbills since I was a kid. These are just a few of my favorites." Now you know that your interviewer has an interest in theater, and it may work well to call on your experiences as an actor in summer stock *if* you can use that information to provide an appropriate benefit that's related to the position for which you are interviewing.

As you can see, research provides a strong reference point for you to be successful in the creative art of presenting relevant benefits. You also need to be flexible and think on your feet. You should use your research appropriately to impress the interviewer with your knowledge and commitment while avoiding the tendency to flaunt the facts you have gathered. "Canned" answers will not get you the job. Appropriate benefits offered at the right time and expressed in the right manner are what you need to get the job you want.

Using Technology to Sell Yourself and Your Skills Even Further

Technology has influenced every aspect of the job search. Today, most companies would prefer that you e-mail your résumé rather than send a paper copy. Video clips now can be attached to these electronic résumés, adding an entirely new dimension to this part of the job search. Phone interviews have become commonplace and often serve as a screening vehicle. E-mail is used to set up appointments, confirm meetings, and provide information. Cell phones, voice mail, and text messaging are all part of our everyday lives, including our work lives.

Don't let the familiarity of these various technologies lull you into complacency. Every interaction you have with a company will be judged during the hiring process. It is vital to integrate your knowledge of features and benefits into your use of technology to ensure a successful job hunt. How you present yourself electronically is as important as how you present yourself in person.

A word about electronic communication: For many companies, e-mail has become the primary means of communication. There is a casualness and immediacy to e-mail that can be extremely valuable during the interview process. Make no mistake, though, even your e-mails will be judged for professionalism during a job search. Choose your words carefully—this is not the time to use Internet shorthand. Write in complete sentences using correct grammar, spelling, capitalization, and punctuation—and *always* end with a benefit of what you can offer the company.

Be aware that humor and sarcasm typically fall flat in an e-mail. You cannot indicate your meaning with tone of voice or a wink and a nod, like you can when you are face to face. Your written message may be misinterpreted for a wide variety of reasons:

❏ The reader is not paying close attention because something else is going on in the room.

❏ The reader may be responding to something that happened just prior to reading your letter or e-mail.

❏ Your reader's interpretation of your message may be colored by an emotional response that you have no way of knowing.

If you have a clever, inappropriate, or overly long outgoing voice-mail message, change it *now* to something more professional. Keep it brief and to the point. Similarly, if your screen name or e-mail address is "Itappakeg" or something equally unprofessional, change it *now.* You should know that companies can and do search the Web for information on potential candidates. Job hunters have lost lucrative offers owing to unacceptable postings on personal Web pages and social networking sites. If it is on the Internet, then it is public property. Protect yourself and your reputation by carefully considering what you say and do on the Web.

Professional blogs, personal Web sites, and online résumés enhanced with video or audio clips can be effective tools in your job search and career. You can update them frequently and provide related links to awards you may have won or articles you have written. Be sure to maintain a high level of professionalism in these and the more conventional forms of communication. And be sure to include your feature/benefit skills to highlight what you have to offer.

THE DAY OF THE INTERVIEW: SOME LAST-MINUTE ADVICE

Anything you can do to help alleviate stress before the interview will help you to be at your best, both physically and mentally. On the day or evening before each interview, double-check everything you need or want to take with you. Get a good night's sleep, and have a decent breakfast. If you will be interviewing late in the day, be sure to eat a healthy lunch before you go.

What to Bring

Be sure to have the interviewer's name and phone number with you. Write down the interviewer's name, and practice saying it. If you are unsure of how to pronounce it, call ahead of time and ask. People like to hear their names, so use the interviewer's name frequently during the interview.

You should also bring a briefcase or portfolio with

- ❏ A pad for notes

- ❏ At least two pens

- ❏ A leather binder holding any awards or letters of recommendation

- ❏ Extra copies of your résumé and a list of references

- ❏ Your business cards

Arrive Early

Plan to arrive at least 30 minutes before the scheduled interview. This will give you time to fill out any required paper work or an application, as well as a few minutes to collect your thoughts and visit the restroom.

Get good directions to the interview site, and find out where you should park. If you will be taking public transportation, be sure you know exactly how to get there and how long it will take. Add at least 30 minutes to your estimated travel time. If at all possible, practice getting to the site *before* the day of the interview. Try to do this at the same time of day as you will be traveling on the interview day to get an idea of traffic conditions and any construction or detours.

If you arrive very early, make sure that you have the right place, and go somewhere nearby to relax or sit in your car and review the information you have. When you go in, introduce yourself to the receptionist, and make note of his or her name. The receptionist is the gateway to the company, and he or she usually knows everyone and everything. You want to make a good impression. Ask where you can hang up your coat, if you have one, and ask for the restroom, if you need one. If the receptionist doesn't appear to be too busy, you might say something casual and open-ended like, "This seems like a nice place to work." Be sure to be polite in all your interactions with the receptionist, and say thank you.

Pay attention while you wait. If the receptionist has the time and inclination to talk, use your questioning skills to learn more about the company. But be sure you are not interrupting or keeping him or her from his or her work.

Meeting Your Interviewer

Carry your briefcase or portfolio in your left hand so that you are free to shake hands with your right. If the interviewer does not greet you by name, introduce yourself as you shake hands (firmly, but not aggressively). Look the interviewer in the eye as you greet him or her, and wait to be asked to be seated.

Making Small Talk

Small talk is just that—small, trivial, and unimportant. Small talk can seem like an easy refuge when you are nervous about an impending interview. That very nervousness may cause you to get caught up in small talk and ramble uncontrollably. Avoid the temptation to initiate irrelevant chitchat because you have no idea how it will be interpreted by the interviewer. Chances are that your interviewer is busy and would prefer to get down to business rather than wasting time discussing the weather or knickknacks in his or her office.

If given the opportunity to initiate the conversation, the best way to open is with a genuine smile and a sincere thank-you for the interviewer's time. Try to talk about something that is relevant to the interviewer: the company's great location, the beautiful offices, the friendly employees, or the helpful receptionist. Be complimentary, and show your interest in the company right from the start.

If the interviewer initiates the small talk, certainly be polite and follow his or her lead, but use it to your advantage. Pay attention to your surroundings, and listen carefully to anything the interviewer says for clues as to what is important to him or her. Remember, your goal is to discover what benefits you can offer that will be meaningful to the interviewer. Think back to that invisible sign on his or her desk asking: "What will you do for *me*?"

The End of the Interview: Taking Your Leave

As the interview draws to a close, you may be tempted to ask, "Where do I stand?" or "What is the next step?" As you have learned, these are closed-probe questions that will not get you real answers. Instead, a question such as "What is the process going forward?" probably will garner more meaningful information, and it even may give you an idea of how the interviewer feels about you.

Make sure to pause and give the interviewer a chance to answer. Pay close attention. If your interviewer asks you to provide some additional information, you need to know when and how to follow up. A request for a work sample faxed or e-mailed by 10 a.m. the next day could be a test of how well you follow directions and whether you can be trusted to meet a deadline. Be sure to respond with the requested information at the stated time and in the required format.

Then shake hands again, and thank the interviewer for the time he or she spent with you. At this point, almost all interview guides will suggest concluding with a statement along the following lines:

❏ "I would really like to work here."

❏ "This seems like a nice place to work."

❏ "I think I could be happy working here."

I disagree with these suggestions. In a job interview, the hiring manager is the customer, and you act as both the salesperson and the product. Think about how *you* would respond in the following situations. For example, if you were buying a car and the salesperson said, "I really want to sell you this car." Or consider if you had to choose a company to repair your roof or fix your plumbing, and the estimator said, "I really want to do this job."

Of course, they want to make a sale or get the contract, just as you want to get the job offer. But what *they* want is irrelevant to you, just as what *you* want is irrelevant to someone interviewing you for a job. In both these examples, the speakers have failed to express any benefits. Even if they talked about price, reliability, experiences, and referrals, they still would not be offering *benefits*. Likewise, the statements listed above and anything similar to them do not offer benefits to the interviewer.

So what *should* you say as you take your leave? Start with something like, "As we discussed, my skills and past experience would make this a beneficial partnership for both of us." Then refer to a specific part of the interview and reiterate the benefit. The knowledge you have gained about what the interviewer values will help you to end the meeting with the most effective benefit.

Also, on your way out, be sure to thank the receptionist again.

AFTER THE INTERVIEW:
EVALUATE HOW WELL YOU THINK YOU DID

After an interview, you are bound to have some mixed feelings. Some things went well, and others felt awkward. You may feel like you have a real chance at a job offer or that you completely blew it. The easy thing to do is to put the entire interview out of your mind and move on to your next chore or start thinking about your next interview.

But experience (good or bad) really is the best teacher. The plain truth is that you probably will fail in an interview more often than you will succeed. Even the best baseball players strike out more often than they get on base. When a batter strikes out, he will review his performance to understand why and be better prepared to face the same pitcher the next time.

Just like the successful ballplayer, it is important to take time after each interview to analyze your performance in detail. Exhibit 8-1 is an "Interview Review Form" to help you evaluate your interview experience. Your review will be most effective if you do it as soon as possible after each interview—while the experience is still fresh in your mind. Ideally, you should complete the form immediately after the interview. The farther you get from the interview itself, the less honest and valuable your responses will be.

Make copies of this form, and use it after every interview. Study it, learn from it, and be better prepared to succeed in the next interview. If you had a successful interview and subsequently receive a job offer, your postinterview review will help you to document what you did well and prepare you for future interviews. If you interviewed poorly, your review will help you to do better next time. As Malcolm Forbes said, "Failure is success if we learn from it."

Exhibit 8-1 SELF-EVALUATION: INTERVIEW REVIEW
FORM

Purpose: To review the things you did right, as well as those areas where you need to make improvements for the next interview.

Write down your general feeling about the interview.
Be honest and use examples. Were you sweaty and
uncomfortable? When? Why?

_____

_____

What did you do well? Rank in order of importance
to a successful interview.

_____

_____

What could you have done better?

_____

_____

What surprised you?

_____

_____

What information do you wish you had before
the interview?

_____

_____

How can you get this information for your next interview?

_____

_____

What did you learn?

_____

_____

What would you avoid in the next interview?

_____

_____

What would you do again?

_____

_____

If you could do the interview over again, what would you do differently?

_____

_____

A Few Words about Rejection and Success

Like it or not, rejection is part of the interview process. Accept the fact that you will be rejected—probably more than once—and embrace each interview as an opportunity to learn more about yourself, the benefits you have to offer, and how to present them in a way that is meaningful to the interviewer. Rejection is just a step on your road to success.

A good portion of this chapter has been devoted to self-evaluation after the interview. Don't skip this step, even if things seemed to go well. If you have been working with a recruiter or a headhunter, get in touch after a rejection and ask for suggestions about how you can improve your interview performance. Recruiters and headhunters often get candid feedback from a hiring company that could be a great help to you.

Ask soft questions to get as much information as possible, and listen carefully to the answers. Take notes. Be sure to thank recruiters or headhunters for their time and assure them that you will heed their advice. A willingness to learn from your mistakes and take proactive steps toward improvement will show recruiters that you are worth their time and effort, and they will be much more likely to send you on future interviews. Remember, your success is *their* success (again, what will you do for *them?*).

Whatever you do, don't give up!

Follow Up with Thank-You Letters

You *must* write a thank-you letter after every interview. Even if you felt the interview was terrible, a prompt and effective thank-you letter can alter the interviewer's ultimate impression of you. If you met with more than one person, you should send an individual note to each interviewer.

Even in this day and age of e-mail, a thank-you letter personally addressed to the interviewer, neatly typed, signed in ink, and sent by regular mail can make a huge positive impression. In some cases, however—for example, if the interviewer stated that she will be making her decision within the next day or two—it will be more important to get your thank-you letter to her by e-mail than to observe the formalities of a traditional letter.

A thank-you note is much more than thanking the interviewer for his or her time. It is another chance for you to emphasize the *benefits* you would bring to the job. Be specific. Repeat all the things that impressed the interviewer during the interview, and if possible, introduce a new benefit that you may have forgotten or been unable to address. Remember, since your meeting, your interviewer has had to attend to other business and probably has conducted other interviews. Therefore, you need to remind your interviewer who you are and what you have to offer. You might want to refer directly to something he or she said, adding new information and benefits: "You mentioned during our interview that you're looking for someone who can hit the ground running. In addition to my 10 years' experience in the field, I have worked directly with some of the same vendors your company uses. These contacts will allow me to be productive from day one."

Even if you gave your interviewer a list of your references at the interview, it is a good idea to include another copy with your thank-you letter. You even may want to include another copy of your résumé so that the interviewer has all your information together in one place. Conclude by thanking him or her again for his or her time and consideration. Proofread all your material carefully for errors before you send it out.

A short thank-you letter to the receptionist or the interviewer's assistant also may be in order. Although an important cog in the company wheel, the support staff is often overlooked. If the receptionist or assistant provided you with any specific help or information, a thank-you note from you will be flattering and may encourage him or her to generate positive buzz about you. He or she is likely to show your note to the person with whom you interviewed because it puts him or her in a good light and will make him or her look good to the boss. Small but important gestures are another way to help you stand out in the crowd.

RATE YOURSELF

To make sure that you've absorbed all the advice given in this chapter, rate yourself again using the worksheet in Exhibit 8-2 on a scale of 1 to 10.

Exhibit 8-2 RATE YOURSELF: DO YOU KNOW WHAT
YOU NEED TO DO BEFORE, DURING,
AND AFTER A JOB INTERVIEW?

Rating (1–10)

- Do I understand the purpose of a résumé, and have I created a targeted résumé for each area and industry in which I intend to interview? _____

- Do I understand how and why I need to do research before an interview? _____

- Do I understand the role of technology in the interview process and how to use it successfully? _____

- Do I understand the importance of arriving early and what I can do to minimize stress before the interview? _____

- Have I made copies of the "Interview Review Form" so that I can use it after each interview? _____

- Do I know how and why to write an effective thank-you letter? _____

Then, if you have given yourself a rating of 7 or better in each of the areas described in this book (using the worksheets at the end of every chapter), you are ready to take your new set of skills to your next interview. There are chapters you may return to again and again throughout your job search.

You certainly will want to use the "Interview Review Form" after *every* interview—to evaluate your performance, to prepare for a second interview, or to work through problems that may have arisen during an unsuccessful interview.

Moreover, you will find that once you have succeeded in getting the job offer you have been looking for, the tools you have learned here will continue to help you beyond the interview in all the following situations:

❏ In your daily interactions with coworkers, supervisors, clients, and vendors

❏ During performance reviews and when you are seeking a raise or promotion

❏ When you become the interviewer yourself—because you will know what benefits to look for in a candidate, as well as how to evaluate his or her ability to communicate those benefits

In short, the skills you have learned will continue to benefit you throughout your career. Good luck!

Index

Abrasive questions, 74
Answering questions, 85–107.
    See also Asking questions
    challenging questions,
      99–103
    dreaded questions, 87–95
    "I wonder if you really can do
      this job," 101–103
    rate yourself, 104–105
    salary conversations, 103–104
    standard questions, 96–98
    "tell me about your former
      boss," 91–92
    turn a weakness into benefit,
      95
    "what are your weaknesses,"
      90–91
    "what part of the job would
      you have trouble with,"
      101
    "why should we hire you,"
      100
    "why were you fired," 93–94

Asking questions
    abrasive questions, 74
    closed probe, 65–72
    leading statements, 76, 80–88
    open probe, 65–72
    prompts, 80–92
    show what you know, 72–73
    soft questions, 73–75, 77–80
    when to ask questions, 76–77

Benefits
    addressing interviewer's
      needs, 15–39
    adjust to suit situation, 23–29
    call attention to, 32–38
    defined, 1
    feature, contrasted, 4
    how to sell yourself letter,
      29–31
    talking about, 11
    turn weakness intostrength, 95
    which are important, 22
Berra, Yogi, 117

Body language, 51–53
Burtch, Linda, 64, 89

Challenging questions, 99–103
Closed probe, 65–72
Communication
    nonverbal, 51–54
Conscious listening, 56–57
Coolidge, Calvin, 41
Cover letter, 138
Coworkers, 124–125

Different interview situations,
    117–136
    benefits from other work/life
      experience, 125
    coworkers, 124–125
    elevator interview, 131–132
    executive recruiter, 118–119
    getting to the next interview,
      120–121
    group interview, 126–127
    headhunter, 118–119
    hiring manager, 121–124
    HR personnel, 120
    in-house recruiter, 119
    job fair, 132–134
    meal interview, 130
    moving up chain of com-
      mand, 124
    rate yourself, 135–136
    second interview, 127–129
    understand the process, 134–135
Dreaded questions, 87–95

E-mail (electronic communication),
    141–143
Elevator interview, 131–132
Elevator interview worksheet, 131
Executive recruiter, 118–119
Eye contact, 53

Facial expressions, 51
Features and benefits
    addressing interviewer's
      needs, 15–39
    benefit, contrasted, 4
    call attention to, 32–38
    combining, with benefits, 10
    defined, 1
    multiple benefits, 21–22
    translating, into benefit, 5–10
Feature and benefit quiz, 4
Forbes, Malcolm, 148
Franklin, Benjamin, 85

Gestures, 51
Group interview, 126–127

Headhunter, 118–119
Hiring manager, 121–124
HR personnel, 120

In-house recruiter, 119
Interruptions, 53
Interview—before, during and
    after, 137–154
    arrive early, 144–145
    cover letter, 138

Interview—*(Cont.)*:
    e-mail (electronic communica-
        tion), 141–143
    ending the interview, 146–147
    meeting the interviewer, 145
    post-interview evaluation,
        148–150
    post-interview rejection/
        success, 150–151
    rate yourself, 152–154
    research the company,
        139–141
    résumé, 137–138
    small talk, 145–146
    technology, 141–143
    thank-you letters, 151–152
    what to bring, 143–144
Interview review form, 149–150

Job fairs, 132–134

Leading statements, 76, 80–88
Letters of recommendation.
    See Networking
Lincoln, Abraham, 15
Listening, 41–62
    conscious, 56–57
    difficulty, 44
    first question to ask, 45
    habit, as, 51
    important words, 55
    notes, 49
    preparation, 46–49
    rate yourself, 61–62

Listening *(Cont.)*:
    record yourself, 59–61
    stop talking, 51
    telephone interview, 57–59
Listening habits rating scale, 50

Meal interview, 130
Mutual trust, 54

Networking, 107–115
    guidelines for references, 112
    maximizing your efforts,
        113–114
    professional/trade association,
        108
    rate yourself, 114–115
    references—ask first, 109–110
    references—make it easy for
        them, 110–112
    thank-you notes, 108

Open probe, 65–72
Open-probe/closed-probe quiz,
    69
Ovid, 11

Peters, Ellis, 1
Phone interview, 57–59
Powell, Colin, 137
Practice
    See also Answering questions
    asking, 83–84
Professional/trade association, 108
Prompts, 80–92

Questions, 63–107.
    See also Asking questions

Rate yourself
    answering questions, 104–105
    asking questions, 83–84
    different interview situations,
        135–136
    interview—before, during and
        after, 137–154
    listening, 61–62
    references, 114–115
References, 109–112.
    See also Networking
Referral, 108.
    See also Networking
Research the company, 139–141
Respect, 54

Résumé, 137–138
Robbins, Anthony, 63

Salary conversations, 103–104
Second interview, 127–129
Selling is Telling, 2–3
Small talk, 145–146
Soft questions, 73–75, 77–80
Sparks, Jared, 45
Standard questions, 96–98

Technology, 141–143
Telephone listening skills,
    57–59
Thank-you letters, 151–152
Thank-you notes, 108

Understanding, 54

About The Author

....

Oscar Adler has 40 years experience interviewing, hiring, and training thousands of sales representatives, sales managers, and sales support staff for Maidenform Brands. He has also coached past offenders with their job search upon their release from jail. Currently, he is principal of Silent Selling where he consults to managers and also counsels job seekers in one-on-one coaching sessions, and small group seminars. He also hosts a local television interview show called *Adler's Alley*. For more information, visit his Web site at www.adlerinterviewtechniques.com